PAT O'BRIEN
TALKIN'

A
B.S.-ER'S
GUIDE

VILLARD
NEW YORK

All rights reserved under International and Pan-American Copyright Conventions. Published in the United States by Villard Books, a division of Random House, Inc., New York, and simultaneously in Canada by Random House of Canada Limited, Toronto.

VILLARD BOOKS is a registered trademark of Random House, Inc.

Grateful acknowledgment is made to Alfred A. Knopf, Inc., for permission to reprint an excerpt from *Days of Grace* by Arthur Ashe and Arnold Rampersad. Copyright © 1993 by Jeanne Moutoussamy-Ashe and Arnold Rampersad. Reprinted by permission of Alfred A. Knopf, Inc.

Library of Congress Cataloging-in-Publication Data
O'Brien, Pat.
Talkin' sports: a B.S.-ers guide / Pat O'Brien.
p.   cm.
ISBN 0-679-77818-7
1. Sports—History. 2. Sports—Miscellanea. I. Title.
GV576.037   1997
796—dc21   97-35856
Random House website address: www.randomhouse.com
Printed in the United States of America on acid-free paper

24689753

First Edition

INTERIOR DESIGN BY ROBERT BULL DESIGN

To Joe O'Brien, who I wish was still around to talk sports. To my wife, Linda, who is the greatest sport of all.

And to Sean Patrick O'Brien, whose dad *is* around to talk sports and, more importantly, anything else.

ACKNOWLEDGMENTS

Research is the mother's milk of sports reporting, and I had four of the best helpers: My trusted assistant, Jaxie Stollenwerck, whose love and devotion for perfection kept us all on the ball. Erin McGuire, whose late-inning maneuvers enabled this book to get out on time. Sean Whalen, who during the course of researching this book hit a home run off my son's baseball team—and pumped his fist (my son is ten years old; the pitcher was nine). Sean, you're the best. And J. K. ("Slice"), who would rather eat pizza and read a sports page than go out with Vendela.

Thanks are also due to:

My literary (this is literary?) agent, Esther Newberg, who is one of the smartest women on the planet.

Don Imus, who taught me a lot about loyalty, and that you *can* have some success in your advancing years.

David Rosenthal, who nursed this book out of the gate, and who probably is still wondering how I finished this project.

All the fans who come up every day and ask if I'll ever be back in sports. I'm in it forever now. I'm in the Library of Congress.

And, finally . . . to all the people who wonder if I take any of this seriously: the answer is, not on your life. Or mine.

INTRODUCTION

There's just no time anymore. No time to watch an entire game. No time to read about it the next day. No time to invest in the heritage of your teams or your sport.

If you agree, this book is for you.

This book is also for you if you are just plain out of town when it comes to sports. I can't tell you how many people have said to me over the years, "You've lost me on that one. The only sports person I know is Michael Jordan." Or the person in the office who comes up to me in a panic, saying, "I'm going to a game tonight, what do I do?" Believe it or not, some people actually lose sleep over this. But not anymore. Help is on the way.

Using this book is simple. You don't even have to read it—just refer to it. Say you are going out to dinner with somebody who knows a whole lot about sports and likes to let everybody know that he or she knows a whole lot about sports. When I was in school we called these people show-offs. At any rate . . . if you are going out in January, turn to the January chapter and stuff away a couple nuggets for ammunition. Or put the book in your pocket and sneak away to the hallway or rest room and quickly memorize something nobody knows about football and come back in, and *BANG!* You're a sports nut.

So have fun. Take the time you don't have anyway to fill up your mind with meaningless facts and figures. It won't improve much of your life, but it'll make people think you're smarter than you are . . . and hey, what's wrong with that?

WHO OR WHAT YOU DON'T WANT TO BE

Have you ever been driving along, minding your own business, when suddenly a Michael Bolton song comes on the radio? You have? Good. So you begin to surf the dial and you hear Rush talking about the same thing he was talking about last week, and you hear Dr. Laura Schlessinger telling some poor guy to dump his girlfriend and become a priest, and you hear some doctor talking about testicular cancer, and none of this particularly interests you. Imus is in a commercial, and so you continue to surf. Then you happen on a sports radio station and, to be honest, you don't realize it because whoever is talking is speaking a language you think is only heard on some Micronesian Island. You listen, and you realize he is talking sports. But not like you or me. He is talking doctorate-level sports. We are here to beg you not to become one of these people. We are here to plead with you to temper your sports knowledge into something entertaining, not become somebody who scratches a blackboard with his fingernails. We are asking you not to take this seriously.

It is okay, for example, to know that Lee Smith saved 30 games or more in nine seasons. But it's not okay to tell somebody that he pitched 1,016 relief innings. That's just too much information.

It's okay to know that Babe Ruth hit 60 home runs in that one magical season in 1927. It's not okay to know that he hit 54 the next year, 46 the next year, 49 the year after that, and then tied Lou Gehrig with 46 in 1931. No. Don't go there.

If you are sitting next to me on a plane and we start talking about, say, jogging, it's actually okay that you can come up with Eamonn Coghlan's world record in the mile of 3:49:78. It's not okay if you add that a mile is really 1,609.344 meters. No no no.

Tell me about Jean-Claude Killy winning the downhill in 1968, but please don't know that Egon Zimmermann won it in 1964. Knowing that Americans Bill Johnson and Tommy Moe won in '84 and '94 shows you bleed Red, White, and Blue, but telling us that Michela Figini and Katja Seizinger won those same years will make me want to spill red wine on you.

In short, you just don't want to be known as a sports geek. There's nothing worse, for example, than the person who name-drops the president's Cabinet at a party or, for that matter, can name at least five cabinet members. Nothing worse than while talking about the economy and in irrational exuberance somebody brings up some vintage Adam Smith or tries to tell you that Robert Samuelson was right all along. Can't put up with the person who can name all the signers of the Declaration of Independence and what happened to them afterward. (Unless you are Paul Harvey, of course.) You just don't want to shock your friends and neighbors unless they turn out to be just as obnoxious and you want to go mano a mano. Here are some more examples:

Take a sport like hockey, which a lot of casual fans don't know a whole lot about. So make sure you know, well, of course, Wayne Gretzky, Mario Lemieux, Eric Lindros, Mark Messier, Jari Kurri, Paul Coffey, maybe Doug Gilmour. And add some old-timers like Bobby Hull, Stan Mikita, Ken Dryden, Gordie Howe, Phil Esposito, and Bobby Clarke. They are all safe names to drop as in "Boy, could Esposito play." Talk about Gretzky's assists. And how about Howe's? But be careful not to throw in a hockey name you're not comfortable with because hockey fans will jump all over you. Oh, don't worry about Kings fans, but those Montreal Canadiens fans will trounce you. So will Toronto Maple Leafs fans. Don't send up a name like George Hainsworth without being prepared to get into a discussion of goals against average during the stock market crash. The key is never to get trapped, but if you do, we have the answer for you in another chapter.

In professional football, it is okay to say something like the following: "You know, I don't think there even was the game of football as we know it today until Joe Namath came along." What you mean here, if pressed, is that Joe added the soap opera and drama needed in professional sports. What you don't want to get involved with is something like "You know, the CFL ought to come down here," and then begin lobbing off Canadian Football League players like old friends. If you know the name Cory Philpot (of the BC Lions) you're going to need some kind of therapy.

Pro football offers good conversation all the way around, however, because it is so popular and people talk about it every single Monday during the season. Listen intently and stay with the flow as sports geeks around the office are talking about that play Jerry Rice made or that pass John Elway executed. You can sit through these conversations like a pro by just using the word "execution," come to think of it. Example: Someone says, "Rice's third catch was a miracle." You say, "I thought it was a simple example of execution." Or someone else says, "I was dumbfounded when Steve Young was rolling left and then right and then he threw!" You say: "Well, football is about execution." Then go on with your business. Other generic things you can *always* say when somebody is discussing football in what seems to be a foreign language:

"It's a tough game, all right."

"Lombardi would have loved that."

"Does anybody wonder if Jim Brown could run through that defense?"

"Those linebackers never used to be that fast."

"I don't know about you, but I'd rather watch a game in Green Bay."

"Does anybody remember San Francisco/Cincinnati? The first game?"

"Bring on basketball."

"I remember when the game was the game."

"Steroids."

"They'll be watching game film all week after that" (after a big loss or terribly executed play).

"You gotta catch those." "You gotta get that yard." "You gotta make that tackle." "You gotta hold onto the ball." And so forth.

When all else fails, say, "I prefer the college game."

Never, never say you prefer the CFL, unless you are a friend of Doug Flutie's or Cory Philpot's.

So make sure of the basics, and while driving, keep the dial on Imus. You understand where we are coming from. It's okay to be *kind of* smart in sports, but you don't want to be a know-it-all, the one who calls into sports talk-radio stations and fills up the airwaves with things you will never, ever use unless you dine with *him,* which is unlikely. So stick to the basics, and, while driving, keep it on Imus. He'll tell you what's *really* important.

Happy New Year. Ordinarily, when a new year comes around it is a time of reflection, renewal, and rebirth. But in the sports world that is reserved for the beginning of baseball—and we'll get to that in another chapter.

In sports January means two things. Football. And more football. And on the very first day of this football month, you will wake up to newspaper headlines screaming about college football. Even in churches around the country, they are talking football with sermons like "Jesus Is My Quarterback," "Touchdown, Jesus," and "It's Not Just a Game." You get the picture.

January is the resolution of the college football season and the beginning of the hype for the Super Bowl. So, in the midst of New Year's resolutions and such, football conversation is in the air.

So it's the first day of the year and your friends are talking football. Some may even have tickets for the Rose Bowl. Certainly, they'll be watching. Someone inevitably will make a remark about how great the weather is each year in Pasadena, the site of the hallowed Rose Bowl. Here's your chance.

JANUARY 1, 1942

The Rose Bowl wasn't played in Pasadena. The game was played in Durham, North Carolina, at Duke University's home field because of fears of a Japanese attack on the West Coast following Pearl Harbor. If you think Pearl Harbor was an upset, how about this: Oregon State beat Duke, 20–16.

If you want to get obnoxious: The Beavers (that's Oregon State) were sparked by two touchdown passes from Bob Dethman, and halfback Donald Durdan was named the game's MVP (Most Valuable Player). This information you would probably use only in the state of Oregon because anyplace else, especially in North Carolina, they just don't care.

Okay, you're watching the Rose Bowl with some friends. (Be sure to check out the chapter on how to watch a game.) The game is going great, and somebody makes a spectacular play that shifts momentum to the opposing team. (Today, the opposing team in the Rose Bowl can only be a PAC 10 team or a Big Ten team.) Here's your chance at glory:

In 1929, California's Roy Riegels turned a game around, but not the way he wanted to. Riegels picked up a Georgia Tech (they let other conferences play in the Rose Bowl before Wall Street crashed) fumble and headed to the Tech end zone. Then, inexplicably, he turned around and began running the wrong way, back toward his own end zone, which is a huge mistake. Well, you can imagine the alumni in the stands watching this in horror. And I'm sure you can imagine what was going on with his *own* team on the field. Finally, a teammate, Benny Lom, with the 70,000-strong crowd going wild, got to him and turned him around at the Cal three, but a gaggle of Georgia Tech tacklers pushed Roy back to his own one. In other words, Cal now had 99 yards to go.

The New York Times headline on Wednesday, January 2, read:

RIEGELS'S 60-YARD RUN TOWARD WRONG GOAL
HELPS GEORGIA TECH WIN ON COAST 8–7.

From that moment on, poor old Roy Riegels was known as "Wrong-Way" Riegels.

OBNOXIOUS POINT
**Who was the guy who fumbled the
ball for Tech? Halfback Stumpy
Thompson. But we don't think many
people paid too much attention to
him after the game. In fact, he
didn't even make some of the
game stories. Benny Lom was
named MVP in the loss.**

Let's say you're watching the Rose Bowl in Brentwood.
You can be either humorous or ironic, take your pick, and say
something like: "Did you guys know O. J. Simpson used to be a
football player?" Laugh, laugh. Then you hit them with a real
situation: January 1, 1969, Ohio State, down 10–0 after an O.J.
80-yard touchdown run, came back to beat USC 27–16 to wrap
up a national championship. That Buckeye team was the last
Big Ten team to win a national championship until Michigan
earned its share in 1998. It was also O.J.'s final collegiate game.
Ohio State has returned to the Rose Bowl eight times since.
USC has returned 12 times. O.J. plays golf at public courses.

The Rose Bowl isn't the only bowl game by the way. Each
year there are roughly 18 to 20. From the Builders Square
Alamo Bowl to the Carquest Bowl to the Jeep Eagle Aloha Bowl
to the Cotton Bowl Classic. The Cotton Bowl, which has been
played in Dallas, Texas, for years, was called by Lindsay Nelson, the colorful play-by-play artist who began every broadcast
with the familiar "Hi, everybody, I'm Lindsay Nelson." By the
way, Lindsay used to wear the ugliest sport coat in the room.

Always. He told me that when he was broadcasting for the Mets, management called him and told him the games were about to go on color television. So he went down to the local haberdashery to buy a couple of sport jackets and saw one that was red and orange and about every pastel color on earth. It was also plaid. He bought it as a joke, thinking he'd stick out on television. The next day, a cabbie yelled out to him, "Hey Lindsay, nice jacket." And the tradition stuck. He once attended the Cotton Bowl Ball in a gold lamé tuxedo. The story here is that they actually made one.

Lindsay was the announcer, by the way, for the 1962 Mets, Casey Stengel's team that had 120 losses in this, the team's first year.

Lindsay also called the Army-Navy game the day Pearl Harbor was bombed. He recalled, "They kept paging guys over the public announcement system. Generals first. Then lieutenant generals. Then captains. By game's end, the stands were empty."

Back to the Cotton Bowl and the play that hard-core Alabama fans will always refer to. It was 1954. New Year's Day. Seventy-five thousand people decided to begin their New Year at a football game. The Classic. Rice's Dicky Maegle was running down the right sideline with the ball. He'd taken off from his own five-yard line. Out of nowhere, off the Alabama sideline, appeared player Tommy Lewis, who illegally ran onto the field, helmet off, and tackled Maegle. He blindsided him at the 42-yard line. The refs gave Maegle credit for a 95-yard touchdown, and Rice went on to win 28–6.

Maegle had a hell of a day. Eleven carries, 265 yards rushing, 3 touchdowns, 24.1 yards per carry. Should you not understand that this is a hell of a day, believe us. It *is* a hell of a day. In fact, you should even say: "He had a hell of a day." The play was voted by the sportswriters back then as the "Sports Odd-ity of 1954." Oh, how times have changed.

The thing about January is that unless you watch the games played in other months, the Hula Bowl, the East-West Shrine Game, and the Senior Bowl in Mobile, Alabama, and no-body does, January is about professional football. It is about the end of the professional football season. It is the beginning of the hype for the Super Bowl, sports' biggest show.

January is also the month of the conference play-off games, which decide who gets to play in the big game. Most of the time, these games are much, much better than the Super Bowl. In fact, it is always safe to complain that the Super Bowl is really never that good. You can say that the two-week layoff and hype wears on the teams. You can say that the AFC sucks. You can complain about lopsided scores. You can complain that you can't get tickets because all the corporations control them. You can complain that the television presentation is out of control, with pregame shows running three, four, or five hours. (I've done a couple myself.) You can complain that the half-time extravaganzas aren't really extravaganzas and should be half the time. You can brag that you don't watch the game, but you do watch the commercials, which are usually the best of the year. But when all is said and done, it is *the* sporting event of the year and a must watch.

But you gotta get there, you say, so here you go.

JANUARY 2, 1982

In an AFC divisional play-off game, San Diego, up 24–0 after one quarter, held off Miami, 41–38, in sudden death. The Pro Football Hall of Fame named it the "NFL Game of the '80s." Chargers kicker Rolf Benirschke nailed a 29-yard field goal to win it in overtime. Both teams combined for 1,036 total yards on offense. Incredibly, reserve quarterback Don Strock led the comeback (Dan Marino was still in college at Pittsburgh) for Miami with four touchdown passes. It was the second consecutive time that a Miami–San Diego game had gone into overtime. Kellen Winslow, so exhausted that he had to leave the game several times because of the South Florida heat, had 13 catches for 166 yards and blocked a Miami field goal attempt on the last play of regulation to send it into overtime. When the game was over, Winslow's teammates had to help him off the field he was so exhausted.

A week later, San Diego fell at Cincinnati, 27–7, in the conference title game. Temperature at game time?? Nine below zero with a windchill of –59 degrees. (You can actually tell this story while you are watching the Rose Bowl under sunny California skies.)

What you should know here is that the conference championships are played on the same day. It is one of the great days in sports. You can compare it to the Saturday at the U.S. Open tennis championships, in which the two men's semifinal matches to determine who plays on Sunday take place. You can compare it to the Final Four in college basketball, the Saturday they play the two semifinal games. (See March.)

At any rate, on the same day San Diego got beaten by Cincinnati, San Francisco hosted Dallas. But the story of this game was one catch. And from this afternoon on, the entire sports world referred to this one catch as "The Catch." Period.

JANUARY 10, 1982

Cowboys and 49ers in the play-offs for the right to play in the Super Bowl. Dallas led 27–21 with 4:54 to play in the game. The ball was on the 49ers' own 11-yard line. In the next four minutes, quarterback Joe Montana led his team down the field, and, with a little more than 50 seconds left, the Niners were on the Cowboys' six-yard line. You remember this as if it happened yesterday. Montana rolled right and hit tight end Dwight Clark for the game-winning touchdown. Final score: San Francisco 28, Dallas 27. Clark's catch was the sixth lead change of the game. Just be assured that this catch was spectacular enough to be called The Catch forever. (See September for another Catch in baseball by another San Francisco resident.)

Things your friends will want to know about The Catch:

- Dwight Clark's claim to fame leading up to The Catch was that he was the boyfriend of Miss Universe, 1980, Shawn Weatherly.

- Dwight Clark was a tenth-round draft choice. This means, basically, that nobody wanted him.

- The play Montana called in the huddle: sprint right option.

- The Catch was the most famous of Joe Montana's 31 come-from-behind wins in his career.

- The fact that The Catch was made against the Cowboys, then legitimately known as "America's Team," helps you anger Cowboy fans.

- Dwight Clark still works for the 49ers. He's reminded of The Catch each and every day of his life.

Stuff about Montana you can throw in:

- Joe met his future wife, Jennifer Wallace, in L.A. when they taped a Schick razor commercial together in 1984.

- As a starter in the regular season, Montana was 117–47. The only team he failed to beat in the regular season was Miami. He lost to the Dolphins twice, although he did beat them when it counted: Super Bowl XIX.

- Thirty-six different players caught his 273 regular-season touchdown passes. His favorite target? Jerry Rice with 55. His second favorite target, at 41, was Shawn Weatherly's former boyfriend.

- Joe was the eighty-second player taken in the 1979 draft. So much for the science of detecting superstars! The number one overall pick that year was that well-known linebacker out of Ohio State Tom Cousineau. You remember Tom, don't you? (This is Tom's last mention, by the way.)

Comeback stories are always fabled.
People who love sports will more often than not tell you about a spectacular comeback, so here's two of the great ones:

First of all, when you talk comebacks, you can always bring up John Elway's name. The Denver quarterback has more fourth-quarter game-winning drives than anybody, including Mr. Montana. He is the comeback kid. When any quarterback on any team is leading his team from behind with the clock running down, you are always safe to compare him with Elway. Never, however, say he's better.

Take your friends back to January 11, 1987. The AFC championship game. This one is simply called "The Drive."

Trailing 20–13 against Cleveland *at* Cleveland Stadium (you can say it was the old Browns' Dogpound), Denver took possession of the ball at its own two-yard line. Elway needed to go 98 yards in 5:32 just to tie the game. He did. In 15 plays. With 39 seconds left in the fourth quarter, Elway threw a five-yard touchdown pass to Mark Jackson and just like that, after the extra point, the game was tied. An airport bar in Denver went wild. Everybody ordered another Coors. In overtime, Elway took the Broncos 60 yards in nine plays to set up the game-winning Rich Karlis 33-yard field goal. Denver went to the Super Bowl.

Stuff about Elway:

- Appropriate that this was called The Drive. John owns and operates several automobile franchises in the Denver area.

- John went to the same college that brought us Tiger Woods, Pete Sampras, John McEnroe, and Chelsea Clinton: Stanford.

- In 1983, the Baltimore Colts drafted Elway, but John didn't want to play there. He told the Colts, and they traded the rights to Denver. Denver's lucky day, don't you think? For the record, Baltimore's a fine town.

- John played baseball in the Yankee minor-league farm system.

- He is 1–3 in the Super Bowl. This bothers him, but not much.

Another comeback story involves an AFC wild-card game in 1993. Buffalo, down 35–3 in the third quarter with nine minutes left, scored an NFL play-off-record 28 points in that quarter and ended up beating Houston 41–38 in sudden death. The 32-point comeback is the greatest in NFL history!

Frank Reich started for Buffalo at quarterback in place of an injured Jim Kelly. It was just the seventh start of his eight-year career. And it was his first start of the 1992 season. Reich was Maryland's quarterback in 1984, when the Terps overcame a 31–0 deficit in the third quarter to beat Miami of Florida and coach Jimmy Johnson 42–40!

There is nothing in sports like the Super Bowl, and it's no co-incidence that it's played on a Sunday. On this particular Sunday, people worship the game and everything about it. It is the one day of the year when even *you* like football. It is certainly the one day of the year when everybody is B.S.-ing about one game. Here are some highlights to make you smarter:

The very first Super Bowl was not called the Super Bowl. Super Bowl I was called the AFL–NFL World Championship Game. It was on January 15, 1967, and, to be honest, not many people cared. The tickets cost only $6, $10, and $12 as opposed to up to $350 now. The Los Angeles Memorial Coliseum was just two-thirds full for the game between Green Bay and Kansas City. The Packers won, 35–10. Bart Starr was the MVP, but you care more about the fact that Vince Lombardi, the legendary Packers coach, was on the sidelines.

NBC televised the game. CBS televised the game. Yes, the game was covered by two television networks. The only game to have the distinction of two distinguished groups of announcers talking all day. Jack Whitaker and Ray Scott did play-by-play for CBS. Frank Gifford (that's Kathie Lee's husband for you nonsports fans) did the analysis. Pat Summerall hosted the pregame. Over at NBC, Curt Gowdy called the action with Paul Christman handling analysis and Charlie Jones coming up with pregame activities. Bob Costas was fourteen and probably watching, I'm thinking, CBS.

Winners picked up $15,000. Losers picked up a check for

$7,500. By comparison, the Packers, in January of 1997, got $48,000 each. You can do the math yourself on why tickets are up to $350 now.

The actual words "Super Bowl" weren't printed on the game tickets until Super Bowl IV. The words were taken from a toy that belonged to the daughter of Chiefs owner Lamar Hunt called the "Super Ball." Lamar liked the name and convinced the National Football League to change "ball" to "bowl," and here we are. If you've ever been to a Super Bowl, you will discover that it's a Super Ball as well—if you have tickets, a way to get to the game, the ability to take a weekend off, enough money to buy the $80 sweatshirts, and so on.

The program for the 1997 Super Bowl cost more than most of the tickets for the first game: $12.

Any Super Bowl discussion should always lead to Super Bowl III. This was the Joe Namath Super Bowl and, in my opinion, the beginning of modern-day sports as we know it. Why? The game had a soap opera attached to it and a genuine leading man.

Joe Willie Namath was a good-looking bachelor seemingly always surrounded by good-looking women. He was the Beatles without music. On a Thursday before the game against the storied Baltimore Colts and their quarterback Earl Morrall, who was filling in for an injured Johnny Unitas, Joe showed up at a news conference with a glass of Scotch in tow and "guaranteed" a victory. Now think about this. He's the quarterback of a professional football team that Las Vegas thinks is an 18 to 20 point underdog. He comes to a news conference with a drink in his hand and tells the world that his team is going to win: "I guarantee it." At that instant, the legend of Broadway Joe skyrocketed and sports crept onto the front pages of the newspapers. Oh yes, and he won the game, 16–7. Joe went 17 for 28 that Super Bowl. Two seasons before that he became the first passer to throw for more than 4,000 yards in a single season. He called some of his passes "bombs," yet in that Super Bowl game, he didn't throw one touchdown pass. The guarantee might have been his best play. In fact it was.

When somebody describes a player's guts, bring up this story because it's tough to find anyone bold enough actually to guarantee a victory the way Joe Willie did. A drink in hand.

In 1987, after the Los Angeles Lakers beat the Boston Celtics, at a celebration after a parade and without a drink in his hand, Pat Riley "guaranteed" that the Lakers would repeat the next season. After *that* celebration, the Lakers literally tied a handkerchief around Riley's mouth.

What made Riley's guarantee so bold? The Lakers were the first team since the 1969 Celtics to repeat. (And what else happened in 1969? Joe Willie Namath's guarantee, of course. Now you're catching on how to B.S.)

Other sports figures who probably guaranteed a victory once or twice: Charles Barkley, Deion Sanders, Keyshawn Johnson, Babe Ruth, Pete Rose, Allen Iverson, and, in his own separate way, Secretariat.

Biggest blunder: Jackie Smith was in the end zone—wide open—if he catches the pass the Cowboys *win*. Instead, the pass from Roger Staubach was right on the numbers, but Smith *dropped* the ball. He was definitely the goat in Super Bowl XIII. Whatever happened to Jackie Smith? You can visit his exhibit in the Football Hall of Fame. Sports *can* be forgiving. Unless you're Bill Buckner.

Tiger Woods award: Doug Williams, the first African-American quarterback to win the Super Bowl, threw four second-quarter touchdown passes. This game was over, basically, at halftime. Final score: Washington 42, Denver 10. This is called a blowout and another reason people started saying: "The Super Bowl is overrated." But we all keep watching.

How to loosen up your team: Joe Montana and his 49ers were on their own eight-yard line and needed a touchdown to beat Cincinnati in Super Bowl XXIII. Joe notices his teammates were a little uptight. He looked over to the sidelines—now this is in the final 3:20 of the game—he looked over to the sidelines and then back into the huddle. He looked over again and then back into the huddle. His team was confused. "Why are you looking out there, Joe?" they asked. Imagine: Super Bowl on the line and Joe was messing around with his team. "Hey, isn't that John Candy standing over there?" Joe asked. They all looked, then said, "Why, yes, it is." "Just wondering," said Joe, who by now had forced his teammates to focus. They went down the field and won.

Joe would later tell me, "Whatever works, works."

Now, football isn't the *only* sport in January —or the only sport you can bring up.

Here's some nuggets you can use at will. When people begin talking about streaks and domination, try this one on them.

JANUARY 19, 1974

In basketball, the Fighting Irish of Notre Dame beat UCLA, 71–70. The story here is that that game ended UCLA's winning streak at 88. These days a big winning streak— I mean a *huge* winning streak—would be 20 games, so think about it. Coincidence: The Bruins began their 88-game winning streak with a win against Notre Dame. This game ended UCLA center Bill Walton's 139-game winning streak.

Another basketball goodie: The Los Angeles Lakers won their thirty-third in a row on January 7, 1972. Led by Wilt Chamberlain and Jerry West, they beat the Atlanta Hawks by 44 points. Coincidence: The Lakers' streak began the same day that their star player, Elgin Baylor, retired from pro basketball.

On the opposite end of the streak deal: On January 7, 1997, Rutgers-Camden beat Bloomfield College 77–72, ending an NCAA record 117-game losing streak.

At a birthday party in January? Nancy Lopez was born on January 6, 1957. She went on to become the first player in LPGA history to win five consecutive tournaments and the first professional, man or woman, to be rookie of the year and player of the year the same season.

JANUARY 31, 1947

Lynn Nolan Ryan, Jr., was born in the town of Refugio, Texas. Ryan went on to hold or share 53 major-league records, including 5,714 strikeouts; 26 seasons; oldest to throw a no-hitter, at 44 years old; first to throw a pitch 100 miles an hour (100.8 mph); threw seven no-hitters.

OBNOXIOUS POINT
Ryan broke Walter Johnson's all-time strikeout record on April 27, 1983, by fanning Montreal's Brad Mills with a curveball.

JANUARY 17, 1942

Cassius Marcellus Clay, Jr., was brought into the world in Louisville, Kentucky. Clay was a seven-to-one underdog before beating Sonny Liston to become the new heavyweight champion of the world in 1964. The writers had said Clay couldn't fight as well as he could talk. Shortly after that, he changed his name to Muhammad Ali and fought and talked his way into being "The Greatest" of all time.

When you're watching the Super Bowl and you see Kareem Abdul-Jabbar in the crowd, you can put this one together. You know, it was in January 1968 when college basketball—as we know it today as a big-time sport—was born. Houston, led by Elvin Hayes and his 39 points, beat Lew Alcindor (that's Kareem before Kareem) and UCLA before a record 52,693 crowd at the Astrodome in Houston, snapping UCLA's 47-game win streak. The game was televised by NBC.

Want to stun your friends?

JANUARY 5, 1971

The Harlem Globetrotters *lost* a game to the New Jersey Reds, 100–99, to snap their 2,495-game win streak.

Also on January 5, but in 1957, Jackie Robinson officially announced his retirement after ten seasons with the Brooklyn Dodgers. He decided to retire because he didn't want to accept a trade to the Giants for $30,000 and a pitcher.

**B.S. FACT OF THE MONTH
THAT CHANGED THE WORLD**
**The Boston Red Sox sold Babe Ruth to their archri-
vals, the New York Yankees, for just over $100,000.
The Yankees went on to be the Yankees. And because
of the curse of the Bambino, the Red Sox went on to
be the Red Sox.**

A nd finally, you're watching a game and your team is scoring
a lot of points and people are giving that team the game.
You say, "On January 31, 1989, in a Division I college basketball
game, U.S. International scored 150 points and *lost* to Loyola
Marymount 181–150."

WATCHING
THE GAME

You've arrived at somebody's house to watch the game. You're terrified. Not only do you not know anything about this game, you don't even know anything about the sport. Someone keeps saying he can't wait to see so-and-so, and you can't wait until the final buzzer. Or is it whistle? At any rate, there you are.

Let's say the sport is basketball. Let's say the game is an NBA play-off. Actually, you can pretty much figure out how to use this stuff with any sport.

One thing you can do early: Bring this book. Excuse yourself every now and then and pick up an anecdote or fact in it and confidently return to your place on the couch.

One thing you can't do is "learn" the sport the day before the game. You'll sound like a fool. So what you do is make sure you get the television on right at the beginning of the broadcast. What sometimes happens is that newspapers, as a little dig at the TV kids, will print tip-off time, not the time the broadcast begins. So the newspaper will say game time is 7:42. What it's leaving out is the 11 minutes that are so crucial to *you*. This is when the announcers lay out the game for you: The analyst lays out the strategy, the play-by-play person gives you historical perspective, and if you have any kind of memory, you can integrate this into your database.

Now the game begins and people in the room start talking about getting into a rhythm. You're wondering right off the bat why anybody is worried early anyway since you've heard that

NBA games are only decided in the last two minutes. This is right if the game is close in the final two minutes. It's true of any game.

Your first level of conversation when you are watching any game is how the superstars are going to do. These are the people who in the end will end up carrying their team or letting it down, so be up on their current stats. Like, Shaq's gotta hit free throws. Jordan's gotta hit his outside shot. Malone's got to play on the road like he does at home. Kemp's got to stay out of foul trouble. Iverson's got to spread the ball around. This kind of thing.

The game is under way, and both teams are shooting well, running up and down the court and answering each other's baskets. It's been a fast-paced game, and the score is within two. You say: "I don't know how they'll be able to keep this up."

Watch away from the ball—"inside in the paint" as they call it—and see if the big guys are bumping around, leaning on each other and so on. No matter what the refs think, you say: "It's going to be a physical game." As the game continues and you haven't heard from the referees, you say: "Did the refs swallow their whistles?"

Some quick notes: Know who's playing. Especially the team names. You don't want to say Rockets when you mean Suns or Jazz when you mean Pacers. This should be a no-brainer, but it happens. Know which team is which. Teams change the colors of their jerseys depending on whether they are at home or on the road. Don't get used to seeing the Lakers only in yellow because suddenly they will be in purple, their road color.

At least know where the teams are in the standings. You don't want to say something like "what a season" when they suck. You don't want to say "what a great season" when you are talking about, say, the 1972–73 Philadelphia 76ers, who went 9–73 that season. So do *some* homework.

Know the teams' current win/loss streak. If a team is on a six-game winning streak, say, "All they have to do is keep this up." If it is on a six-game losing streak, say, "Things gotta change sometime."

Whistle blows. Commercial. The gang's first real discussion of the game usually turns to the announcer. If it's Dick Engberg, you'll want to say, "I love it when the veterans are at the game." If it's Mike Breen, say, "Have you heard him on Imus? Do you think he's funnier than Warner?" If it's Dick Stockton, say, "He's a game guy." If it's Chick Hearn, look ahead to March. But you know what? It doesn't really matter because at this level there are good and bad, so you'll have to live with it. It's always fun to pick on the announcer, though. Here's some subjects *off* the court you can rely on:

1. **Hair.** Many announcers have toupees. Many don't and should. Some have done plugs with disastrous results. Some have seventies hair. Some don't have hair but have shine. And many, maybe including me, have through the years tried various colors.

2. **Clothing.** When they get away from the blue blazers and ugly ties, many announcers get into trouble. Usually the studio guys have clothing deals, so they always look as if they just went shopping. A tan Joseph Abboud suit at courtside sometimes looks a little pretentious. So always applaud the blue blazer and laugh about the ties later.

3. **Screaming and hyperbole.** I was once in a hotel room surfing channels and stopped on a game where the announcer was screaming that it was close. It was 2–0. Screaming is allowed, in my book, only at the end of the game, when somebody hits a game-winning buzzer-beater. The rest of it is a

waste of vocal cords. And hyperbole: A guy makes a spectacular steal, runs it down the floor, and fires it, without looking, behind his back to another player. The announcer goes wild. But, in fact, it's a set play; they've practiced it forever. Now, a 50-foot shot at the buzzer is another thing.

4. **Getting the names right.** There's nothing more irritating than calling a player by a wrong name. I'll show you my mail.

5. **Silence.** Great on TV. Bad on radio.

6. **Not letting your analyst talk.** There are some play-by-play guys—and you'll figure them out—who love the sound of their own voice and *never* let the other guy talk. That's why the other guy is always so irritated once he gets the chance.

Later in the game, there are definite things you can watch for: When you see players hanging on to the bottom of their shorts, they are so tired they can't hold their arms on their own. This is something coaches look for. You can bet the guy goes out soon.

Late in the game—a close game—you want the ball in the hands not only of your best player but of your best free-throw shooter. Not always guys like Wilt Chamberlain and Shaquille O'Neal.

Player gets ball and shoots quickly from three feet and misses.
You moan.

Player gets ball and shoots quickly from three feet and makes it.
You say, "He's got that shot in him."

Guy hits two jump shots in a row from top of the key.
You safely say, "That's his game."

Guy drives to the hoop and gets shot down.
You say, "Don't go in there."

Little guy drives to the hoop and makes a great layup.
You say, "Wilt never let those guys in there."

Guy who misses free throws didn't finish college.
You say, "He should have finished college."

Guy fouls out and throws something.
You say, "Tough life making ten million dollars."

Fight ensues.
You make hockey reference: "I went to a fight and a basketball game broke out."

Coaches clear benches.
You wonder if they are thinking about wardrobe.

Fans start booing and you don't know why.
You say, "I can't believe it, either."

Fans in stands start doing the wave. You ask if anybody knows who invented the wave?
The answer is Robb Weller, former host of *Entertainment Tonight.*

Everyone in the room groans at the same time. They've seen something you haven't. You either ask, "What happened?" and when they say, "illegal defense," you say, "I thought so. They have to learn how to make that look like man-to-man." You never say, "I don't get it." Just shake your head and agree. If it's an incredibly bad call and everybody is beside himself, just scream, "Bartender!" This always relaxes everybody and shows that you, too, are incredulous.

Game ends. At this point, you should know who plays who next. For example, if the Lakers win, you say, "We're on to

Utah." Or if the Lakers lose, you say, "Let's hope the Western Conference can bring it home."

If it is one of those games for the ages—and they'll let you know—don't ever say, "I could have had floor seats to this, but I thought you wanted to watch it on television."

If the game ends and you see people crying because they lost, console them with "It's only a game. Maybe next year." If they're crying because they won, before you hang out with them again, ask them this: "What was the last book you read?"

February

With January behind you and your Super Bowl ré-sumé now stocked with some stories, you are on your way to tackle a couple of other sports. And February gives you a chance to go against the greatest sports snobs ever: baseball fans. There is so much baseball lore and so many statistics it is impossible for anybody, really, to keep up. So our advice is to tuck away a couple of important pieces of trivia and hold it at that. Warning: You're never, ever, going to sit down with a baseball snob and win. It just doesn't happen. They are like wine snobs. Lovable in their own way but impossible to argue with.

In short, February is your month of renewal because of the very fact that baseball players report to their spring training camps. What this means with the B.S. is that all is well with the world again. The national pastime has begun anew. All the mistakes and the losses and the heartaches of the seasons past are history (unless you follow the Chicago Cubs or the Boston Red Sox). When you hear the crack of the bat and the sound of the ball hitting the mitt, your blood feels red again. You're an American, by God, and whether you like it or not, you're a base-ball fan.

Obviously, you are not—because you are reading this chapter—so we'll try to help you along as February rings in the sport invented by Abner Doubleday. (Actually, even *that* is in dispute because back in 1905, a committee commissioned by Albert G. Spalding, a pioneer in the game, claimed that Abner Doubleday did invent the game, but even old Abner did not write in any of his diaries that he invented it. Some say there might have been two Doubledays. So why give it to Doubleday? Just say, "That's baseball.") It's a kids' game, played by adults who pretend to be kids.

And I'll guarantee you, kids know more about this sport than they do about Magellan. But that's another story. That's baseball. In fact, you can say, "That's baseball" just about anytime there is something confusing or exciting about the game—or life itself. If there's a play that is so difficult to figure out or there's a double switch late in the game that turns out to be successful, just say, "That's baseball." If your favorite player is traded for somebody you never heard of, let's say it together: "That's baseball." If for some reason the Chicago Cubs win the pennant. That's baseball. If Albert Belle starts granting personal one-on-one interviews. That's baseball. A batter with a .224 average gets $7 million a year. That's baseball. You get it now, don't you?

At any rate, February means the start of spring training. They call it the Grapefruit League in Florida and the Cactus League in Arizona. Don't just let people walk all over you on this one. The word "grapefruit" is based on the fact that Florida is a prime growing area for citrus fruit. "Cactus" is taken because of the cacti that are common in the part of the country where Arizona sits. Or, that's baseball.

Your sports-savvy friends are talking about the fact that "pitchers and catchers are reporting to camp." *You* can begin with the fact that the first team to train in Florida was the Washington Statesmen in 1888. Those fellas went to Jacksonville.

Here's a bunch of good February stories you can impress your friends with.

Did you know, you'll ask them, that two of baseball's greatest home run hitters were born in the month of February? On February 6, 1895, George Herman "Babe" Ruth was born in

Baltimore. The "Babe" went on to hit 714 home runs in his career. He hit 15 of those in World Series.

The Babe compiled a lifetime average of .342 and was 94–46 with a 2.28 ERA as a pitcher.

Your friends are talking about Mantle and Maris and Aaron and you're telling them Babe Ruth was the first player to hit 30, 40, 50, and 60 home runs in a season. And think about this: In 1927, on arguably the greatest Yankee team ever, with the fabled Murderers' Row, Babe hit 60 home runs. Was he the MVP of that team? No. It was Lou Gehrig. That's baseball.

In case you've moved right to the February chapter and didn't read January, where the Bambino is also discussed, Ruth began his career with the Boston Red Sox and was traded to the New York Yankees right before the 1920 season. How much? A hundred grand. You couldn't buy a hitter's publicist today for a hundred grand. Ruth finished his career in 1935 with the National League's Boston Braves.

A guy named Emil Fuchs had signed Ruth to become a part-time player for a mere $25,000. In one of his final games with the Braves, he hit homers 712, 713, and 714 against Pittsburgh. Just over a week later, he said good-bye to baseball.

We later found out that many of the legendary stories about Babe Ruth are the stuff of legends only, but nobody seems to care. He was bigger than life, and so are the stories.

Here's one that is true. Reggie Jackson showed me a baseball once signed "To Reggie, your friend The Babe." Since Babe Ruth died in 1948, I quickly computed that this was impossible. It turns out that Babe Ruth used to sit around and sign a number of balls to John, to Sam, to Jim, and so on and finally got around to a couple to Reggie. Somebody bought it at an auction for Mr. October.

Almost 39 years to the day after Babe Ruth was born, Henry Aaron was born, on February 5, 1934. Babe's career was winding down—his last full season was in '34—and now here came Hank Aaron. Aaron slugged a major-league record 755 home runs over his brilliant 23-year career. He piled up 3,771 hits and played in 24 major-league All-Star Games, including the years 1959, 1960, and 1962, when two All-Star Games were played. (This is why in 23 years, he could play in 24 All-Star Games. That's baseball.)

Hank Aaron holds more major-league batting records than any other player in the game's history. His most famous home run came on April 8, 1974, when he hit an Al Downing 1–0 fastball over the fence in Atlanta to break Babe Ruth's all-time home run record. Downing, a lefty for the Dodgers, will always be an answer to one of baseball's best trivia questions, so there you go.

OBNOXIOUS POINT
Wanna be obnoxious? Braves relief pitcher Tom House caught the record-breaking hit in the left-field bull pen.

Your baseball friends will have a million stories about Joe DiMaggio, who on February 7, 1949, signed a new deal to play baseball with the New York Yankees, making him the very first $100,000-a-year baseball player. (He was first offered $90,000, but a buddy of his, legendary New York saloon owner Toots Shor, talked him into a hunskie.) The Yankee Clipper was considered the greatest center fielder of the modern baseball era. He was the American League's MVP three times, and his streak of 56 consecutive games in which he got a hit is considered by many an unbreakable record.

After he signed his big deal with the Yankees, he played only three more seasons.

Stuff you already know about DiMaggio:

He was married to Marilyn Monroe. Once, after Monroe had returned from a visit overseas to our armed forces, she said to her baseball superstar husband: "Joe, you never heard such cheers." He replied, "Yes I have."

He changed the way people endorsed products and the way people got themselves awake in the morning by becoming Mr. Coffee for the machine with the same name.

One of the most famous lyrics of the sixties was from Simon and Garfunkel: "Where have you gone, Joe DiMaggio, our nation turns its lonely eyes to you." But you knew that.

Also in February, on the third in 1979, the Minnesota Twins traded seven-time batting champion and 1977 American League MVP Rod Carew to the California Angels for pitchers Brad Havens and Paul Hartzell, outfielder Ken Landreaux, and infielder/catcher Dave Engle. Why is this a big deal? Because at the time it was a *huge* trade. You trade your seven-time batting champ? Carew went on to play some good years with California and collected his three-thousandth hit against Minnesota. He went into the Hall of Fame on the first ballot in 1991.

Dave Engle's claim to fame? He had the first hit (a home

run) in the history of Minnesota's Metrodome, on April 6, 1982.

More baseball in later chapters. It is our national pastime, after all.

But a couple more baseball birthdays in February.

FEBRUARY 14, 1913

Mel Allen, one of the greatest voices in baseball, who invented "going, going, gone" for a home run call. And when you hear Chris Berman cry out "back, back, back, back, back" for his home run calls, you can say, "As Mel Allen used to say, 'How about that.' "

FEBRUARY 17, 1908

Red Barber, New York City's very first radio announcer and very first television announcer in baseball, worked for the Brooklyn Dodgers and the New York Yankees. He did the first baseball telecast on station W2XBS, for you B.S.-ers game one of a doubleheader between the Dodgers and the Reds at Ebbets Field. There were 400 television sets in New York at the time. The Reds won. Nobody checked the ratings.

Barber was behind the mike when Roger Maris broke Babe Ruth's single-season home run record, and he was there when Jackie Robinson took the field to break baseball's color barrier.

Barber and Allen were the first broadcasters allowed into the Baseball Hall of Fame.

OTHER FEBRUARY BIRTHDAYS YOU CAN TOAST TO

Greg Norman, the golfer. John McEnroe, the tennis player. "Dr. J"—Julius Erving—the basketball player. All *greats* in their sports. I wouldn't say Michael Jordan, the basketball player, though. It just wouldn't be right. Just say he's the greatest ever and let the sports experts in your presence argue. As for John McEnroe, you might throw this one out: "You know, I think McEnroe got some really B.S. calls. I don't blame the guy." As for Norman, say this and watch the sparks fly: "The Masters isn't that big a deal." And Julius Erving? "Hey, all he could do was dunk." Just some conversation starters.

Speaking of Dr. J, he was born Julius Winfield Erving II, on Washington Irving's birthday in 1950, and his mother was urged to name him Washington Erving, but she wisely settled for Julius. Doc was elected to the Basketball Hall of Fame in 1993 as one of the game's greats and one of sports' most respected ambassadors.

Take this stuff with you next time you're in Philadelphia.

Signed as a free agent by the American Basketball Association's Virginia Squires after his junior season at UMass, Erving went on to play 16 seasons in the ABA and NBA. He was an ABA MVP twice and shared the honor in 1975 and played in five ABA All-Star Games. On October 20, 1976, his contract was sold by the New York Nets to the Philadelphia 76ers. He went on to play 11 seasons in Philadelphia, winning NBA MVP honors in 1981 and leading the Sixers to a title in 1983. He appeared in the NBA All-Star Game in each of his 11 seasons in Philly, capturing the MVP Award twice. In his combined ABA/NBA regular-season career, he averaged 24.2 points a game on 51 percent shooting along with 8.5 rebounds and 4.2 assists a game. Erving is one of three pro players (Kareem Abdul-Jabbar and Wilt Chamberlain are the others) to score over 30,000 career points.

In 1984, the season after Doc's first and only NBA title, the Sixers went down hard at the hands of the New Jersey Nets in the first round. After the game, I went into the locker room, which was in a state of shock. Guys were crying. Guys were throwing garbage cans. Guys were taking blame, pointing fingers. It was a mess. I asked somebody where Dr. J was, and they silently pointed to the shower area. There he was. Already dressed. Tying his necktie and whistling. I asked him how he felt about the loss, and he said: "Not great, but I look at it this way. I've got another two weeks with my family." Doc could always put things in perspective.

We told you about Ruth and Aaron, baseball's two "Sultans of Swat," being born in February. The two "Barons of Basketball" were also born in February. Julius Erving and a child who came to us on February 17, 1963. His name is Michael Jeffrey Jordan. Something in the air in Brooklyn? That's where MJ was born, along with two other players who were responsible for taking the game of basketball above the rim: Connie Hawkins and Julius.

If we went into the Jordan story, this book would end up being about the greatest player in the game. So here's some things your friends will claim they've heard but probably haven't.

They will tell the old joke that Dean Smith, Jordan's coach at North Carolina, was the only person to hold Jordan to under 20 points. But you can say that "under Dean Smith's system, there was no superstar system. You were on the team. They were not on your team." So if Michael only averaged 20 points, it made him a good team player, certainly good enough for a national championship in 1982 against Georgetown. And who took the winning shot? You're right.

MJ was cut as a sophomore at Laney High School in Wilmington, North Carolina. The coach who picked one of Jordan's childhood friends, a 6'7" sophomore named Leroy Smith, over Michael was named Clifton Herring. Jordan, at the time, was an inch under six feet. But he could dunk.

When Jordan was a senior in high school, a kid named Buzz Peterson beat him out as North Carolina High School Player of the Year.

His teachers told Jordan to go into math because that's "where the money is."

His dad's passion was baseball.

When Michael was 12 years old, he pitched the Wilmington team to within one game of advancing to the Little League World Series. He threw a two-hitter in the East Regional title game but lost 1–0.

Michael's brief career with the Birmingham Barons is now legend. Watch *Space Jam*. But if you want to throw something out there for the know-it-alls, his first home run for the Barons was in 1994. It was a 380-foot shot off Carolina Mudcats pitcher Kevin Rychel. Nobody saw the home run for two days. That's how long it took to find a video of the thing. No television crew was covering the game.

What do Michael and Sam Bowie have in common? Bowie was the second pick in the 1984 NBA draft. Hakeem Olajuwon was first. Michael ended up third with the Chicago Bulls, who also drafted track star Carl Lewis in the tenth round.

Michael and Carl Lewis have something else in common: They both have Olympic gold medals.

By the way, if you are ever in a situation where somebody around you throws a chair in February, note that on February 23, 1985, Indiana coach Bob Knight and his Hoosiers were playing Purdue. He protested a call and got a technical foul. As the Boilermakers were shooting free throws, his anger came full circle. Knight picked up a chair and flung it onto the court. The replay of this incident is still shown but, as far as we know, not at any basketball training camps for kids.

Everybody has heard of Wilt Chamberlain's 100-point game, but it was February 13, 1954, when Furman's Frank Selvy set an NCAA Division I record with 100 points against Newberry. It was a home game in Greenville, South Carolina, and his mom had made the trip to watch her son perform. Did she get her money's worth? Yes. He hit 41 field goals and 18 free throws. Just three minutes into the game, the player assigned to guard Selvy fouled out.

Just 11 days earlier, on the second, Clarence "Bevo" Francis scored an NCAA record for all divisions when the Division II player scored 113 points for Rio Grande against Hillsdale. You can safely say two things. Not many on his team showed up for the game. Rio Grande had 134 points total, 113 in Francis's column. And you can very safely say that Hillsdale needed work on its defense. Have you ever heard the words "double-team"?

Although football isn't played in February, there has been a lot of football history made in this month. The great football fans of Green Bay, Wisconsin, can certainly attest to this.

FEBRUARY 1, 1968

Legendary Packers head coach Vince Lombardi resigned as head coach after nine seasons on the sidelines. Lombardi won two Super Bowls and five NFL championships. Lombardi's Packers teams won nine of ten play-off games, and his record as head coach was a gaudy 98–30–4, with a .758 win percentage. He stayed on in 1968 as the Packers' general manager before resigning to become part owner, executive vice-president, and head coach of the Washington Redskins. Lombardi led the Redskins to a 7–5–2 record in the fall of 1969. On September 3, 1970, Vince Lombardi died at age 57 from cancer.

On that same date in 1950, Earl "Curly" Lambeau, founder of the franchise and Green Bay's head coach since the team's inception in 1921, resigned under fire. Lambeau won 212 games in his tenure as the Packers' head man. Green Bay's current stadium was renamed Lambeau Field in 1965 following his death.

FEBRUARY 5, 1942

We already mentioned many sports greats born in February, but let's not forget "Roger the Dodger." Roger Staubach, former U.S. Naval Academy and Dallas Cowboys great, was born on February 5, 1942, in the Queen City, Cincinnati, Ohio. Staubach acquired his nickname because of his great scrambling ability. After winning the Heisman Trophy in 1963 as a quarterback at Navy, Staubach was drafted by the Cowboys. After fulfilling his military obligations, Staubach joined Dallas in 1969 and wasted little time making his presence known. In 11 seasons in Big D, Staubach led his team to six NFC championship games, four Super Bowl appearances, and two Super Bowl titles. Twenty-three times over his storied career, Roger led Dallas from behind to win the game, including

14 times in the last 2 minutes of overtime. A five-time Pro Bowl selection, Staubach retired in 1980. Five years later, he was inducted into the Pro Football Hall of Fame in Canton, Ohio.

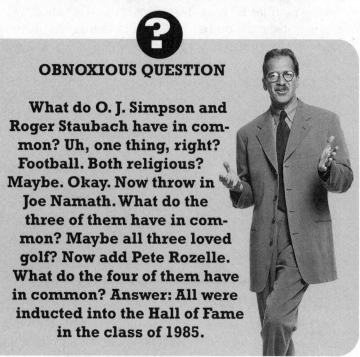

❓ OBNOXIOUS QUESTION

What do O. J. Simpson and Roger Staubach have in common? Uh, one thing, right? Football. Both religious? Maybe. Okay. Now throw in Joe Namath. What do the three of them have in common? Maybe all three loved golf? Now add Pete Rozelle. What do the four of them have in common? Answer: All were inducted into the Hall of Fame in the class of 1985.

Other football history occurring in February: On February 8, 1936, University of Chicago halfback Jay Berwanger became the first player ever selected in the NFL draft. Berwanger's rights were ultimately traded to the Bears, but Berwanger never played a down of pro football in Chicago or anywhere else for that matter.

FEBRUARY 15, 1978

Twenty-four-year-old Leon Spinks, fresh out of the amateur ranks, knocked off Muhammad Ali in a 15-round split-decision win. Spinks got $320,000 for the fight, and Ali got $3.5 million! Ali outweighed Spinks by 17 pounds, but that didn't faze the 1976 Olympic light heavyweight champion. Going into the bout, Ali was such a heavy favorite that legal bookmakers in Las Vegas didn't even put down odds on the fight.

FEBRUARY 2, 1997

The University of Nebraska doesn't only contribute great football players to the sports world: On February 2, 1997, Jeremy Sonnenfeld, a sophomore at Nebraska, achieved perfection in the sport of bowling. Sonnenfeld, from Sioux Falls, South Dakota, rolled the first sanctioned 900 series in the 101-year history of the American Bowling Congress. He rolled three consecutive 300 games during a Young American Bowling Alliance–sanctioned tournament at the Sun Valley Lanes in Lincoln, Nebraska. Sonnenfeld used a 16-pound Columbia 300 Pearlized Blue Pulse Ball in this historic feat. His previous best had been 826, which he got twice. He will be forever known as "Mr. 900." This one you can tell right after you take a pull from a cold tall one.

OBNOXIOUS POINT
According to a 1997 survey, over 53 million Americans bowl.

Beginning with the Daytona 500, the Super Bowl of auto racing, February marks the beginning of the NASCAR season. On February 14, 1988, 50-year-old grandfather Bobby Allison held off his son, Davey, by a couple of car lengths to win his third and last Daytona 500. The two went fender to fender, bumper to bumper, before the elder Allison finally pulled away on the last lap to win. Davey did have his day in the sun at Daytona though, winning the 1992 500. The next year Davey's helicopter crashed at Talladega Superspeedway, and, just like that, Davey Allison was gone. He was thirty-two.

FEBRUARY 18, 1979

Another memorable Daytona 500 moment: Richard Petty, stock car racing's greatest ever, won his sixth Daytona 500. Petty took the lead on the last lap after Donnie Allison and Cale Yarborough crashed, knocking Allison out of the lead spot. It was Petty's first win in 46 races. Petty had lost the 1976 Daytona because of a crash yards from the finish line. "King Richard," as he was called, was driving against his doctor's orders and with only a third of his stomach remaining after an ulcer operation. Petty finished his 34-year-career with a record 200 NASCAR wins and seven Daytona 500 titles.

OBNOXIOUS QUESTION
Who won the first-ever Daytona 500, in 1959? Lee Petty, Richard's father. Richard's son, Kyle, is currently on the NASCAR circuit.

February is also the month of the Winter Olympics and some of the world's favorite sporting moments. There is so much Olympic history, it is virtually impossible for any human being—indeed, even any superknowledgeable baseball fan who knows it all—to keep up. So everybody needs a base of information just to stay close to the Olympic aficionado.

In reality, it's not as difficult as you might imagine. The events are on television one at a time, so you only have to know one thing at a time. Here's how you operate during the Winter Olympics. You go by what you're looking at, and we begin with the opening ceremony.

First of all, it's not opening ceremonies. It's ceremony. There's only one. You can trap anybody with this one, so go ahead.

You're watching the opening—what is it?—ceremony—and you see nearly 70 countries and nearly 2,000 athletes (in 1994 in Lillehammer, Norway, it was 67 countries and 1,737 athletes) and you think back to the very first Winter Olympics in 1924, in Chamonix, France. Sixteen countries and 258 participants. You're smart enough to build on this piece of information, like you can't believe how much it's grown and so on. In 1924, the United States won one gold medal. Charles Jewtraw brought home a gold in the 500-meter speed skating, which sets the stage for your Olympic knowledge base. You're gonna stick with ice.

The embodiment of a Winter Olympics win took place in Lake Placid, New York, in 1980. Ice hockey. Twenty years after the only other U.S. Olympic gold in hockey in Squaw Valley, California, the U.S. hockey team came up with a dramatic gold medal performance that captivated not only Americans but the free world as we knew it then.

It was February 22, 1980, George Washington's Birthday. The United States beat the USSR squad 4–3. We were trailing 3–2 entering the third and final period. U.S. team captain Mike Eruzione scored the eventual game winner on a wrist shot past goalie Vladimir Myshkin. That made it 4–3. Mark Johnson had tied the game at three on a power play.

But the key here is, after the U.S. beat the USSR, there was *still* another game to play because this was only the semifinals. People to this day will say that the United States beat Russia to win the gold. Not so. We had to play another game—this one against the Finland team—in the finals. The Red, White, and Blue came out on top there, and a national celebration ensued. Just as in the Soviet Union win two days earlier, the Americans trailed by a goal, but we outscored them 3–0 in the third and the rest is history.

In the U.S.'s final two games, the semis and the final, they outscored their opponents 5–0 in the third period, 2–0 against the USSR and 3–zip against Finland.

MEMORABLE MOMENTS

ABC's Al Michaels just before the buzzer in the Russian match. "Do you believe in miracles? Yes."

Goalie Jim Craig, with a flag draped around his shoulders and tears running down his cheeks, looking for his father, who had been recovering from an illness, in the stands.

That U.S. Olympic team went to Lake Placid completely unknown outside esoteric hockey circles and came back to parades and sedan chairs.

FEBRUARY 23, 1980

Among the spectators that Friday night when the U.S. beat the Russians was a kid named Eric Heiden, who walked through the crowd nearly unnoticed. The next day he shattered the world record in the 10,000-meter speed-skating event, beating the record by more than six seconds. Heiden became the first-ever athlete to win five gold medals at one Winter Games. You have to marvel at this accomplishment every time you see somebody step up to the podium to get any medal. Five in one Olympics. He had conquered the gold in the 1,500, the 1,000, the 5,000, and a 500-meter sprint only eight days earlier.

Your listeners are trying to soak this in when you put it into perspective. This would be like a track racer winning sprints at 200 and 400 meters, the middle distances at 600 and 800, and then the mile. Just not going to happen.

Eric was only 21. He also set Olympic records in each of his events. As you watch the Olympics and watch people *try* to set records or come close, bring that one up. That year Eric won the James E. Sullivan Award as the nation's outstanding amateur athlete.

The big note here is that Eric didn't cash in on his five gold medals. He was, by nature, not the kind of person who wanted to go out and earn millions off his accomplishments. He went on to live a quiet life in Palo Alto, California, became a doctor, and road-bikes for a hobby.

But the kid was *big* in Europe, as most Winter athletes are. In fact, after the Olympics, one of the most popular songs in Norway was "The Ballad of Eric Heiden." Back in the States "We Are Family" was sweeping the country and every good old-fashioned American family claimed Eric Heiden as part of its life.

Stick with the ice.

As you watch figure skating, it is always safe to bring up Katarina Witt, who continues to be the diva on ice. On February 27, at the '88 Olympics in Calgary, Katarina Witt won the gold. She was representing East Germany, who we later found out was spying on her—everything from what was in her refrigerator to who was in her bed. Witt became the first woman figure skater since Sonja Henie to win a gold medal in two consecutive Winter Olympic Games. Henie, from Norway, was 15 when she won her first figure-skating title at the 1928 games at St. Moritz, Switzerland. She also won gold at the '32 and '36 games. Her streak had to end because the Winter Olympic Games were discontinued until 1948! Henie made her Olympic debut at the 1924 Games in Chamonix. At age 11, she finished last in the competition.

The queen of American gold medalists is Bonnie Blair. In 1994 in Lillehammer, when she won a gold medal in the 500-meter speed skating, she became the first in her sport to win the same event and a gold medal in three consecutive Olympic games. Like Eric Heiden, she has five Olympic golds, including two in the 1,000 meters.

Blair is the only American woman to win five Olympic golds in the Winter or Summer games. The pride of Champaign, Illinois, she is sometimes overlooked in this world of glitz and glamour, but in the world of Olympic glamour she is *it*. She retired on her thirty-first birthday as reigning world sprint champ. Like Eric Heiden, who also didn't cash in, she is one of the nicest persons to ever walk the face of the Earth.

Dan Jansen. His heartache at the Olympics has been well chronicled. He fell on the ice in 1988 at the Calgary games after learning of his sister's death from leukemia. He fell apart in Albertville, France, in 1994, and, in 1996, on the verge of becoming the Buffalo Bills of figure skating, finally won a gold on his last Olympic race. He picked up his kid and did a victory lap with his family while the rest of us were crying.

As you listen to Dick Button comment on figure skating leading up to the Olympics, there are several ways to remember him. For one thing, nobody performed compulsories better than he. Compulsories are figure eights. In case you ever forget that he was better than anybody else in this technical aspect of skating, Dick will be happy to remind you.

Nevertheless, Dick became the first American to win an Olympic gold medal in figure skating, in 1948. During his program he landed the first double axel in competition. Button became the first skater ever to perform a triple jump in competition when he won his second gold medal in 1952. Even though famed Olympic chronicler Bud Greenspan does not put Dick in even his Top 100 Olympic moments, Dick did win seven straight national championships from 1946 to 1952 and five straight worlds from 1948 to 1952. He was—for his time—a great one.

A February Olympics would not seem possible without seeing Alberto Tomba of Italy come racing down the slopes. Alberto is not only the class of Alpine events, he is also the Olympics' biggest playboy. He'd arrive—usually late and always with a huge entourage—in his own helicopter, blowing snow all over the other competitors. With the day done and Alberto usually winning, he would let everybody else go back to the Olympic Village while he closed down every club in the surrounding villages. He is one of a kind.

He won the gold in 1988 in the slalom and giant slalom in Calgary. He is the all-time Olympic alpine medalist with five. He became the first Alpine skier to win gold medals in two consecutive Winter Games when he won two events in the 1988 games and the giant slalom in 1992.

You don't talk gold, money, machismo, women, or wine without uttering the name Alberto Tomba.

SHORT STUFF YOU CAN USE

During figure skating, bring up Tonya Harding's attempt on Nancy Kerrigan's life in Detroit before the Lillehammer games. Well, it really wasn't attempted murder, but she was behind the plot to mess up her knees. Bonus name: Shane Stant was the fat guy who was the club man in what was known as "the gang who couldn't club straight." They were all caught, and Tonya went on to be the National Freak Show while Nancy became America's sweetheart. One's a mom, and the other's been kidnapped once or twice.

During men's figure skating, bring up the fact that Paul Wylie was going to retire and return to Harvard after just showing up in Albertville. Instead, he skated the program of his life, won the silver, and is still skating.

OTHER FEBRUARY HAPPENINGS
WORTH DROPPING

February 9, 1992 — Magic Johnson's comeback at the All-Star Game after he announced he was HIV positive. He was MVP and scored 25 points.

During All-Star weekend in Miami in 1990 . . . on the other side of the world in Tokyo, Jim Lampley said the following words, which shocked the world: "Mike Tyson has been knocked out." Buster Douglas went from a nobody with no plan to heavyweight champion of the world.

Jerry Jones bought the Dallas Cowboys in February, which gives you a very nice Valentine's Day toast in the month. You have to mention, however, that he promptly fired "America's Coach," Tom Landry.

THE FIRST TIME

Going to your first sporting event can be as stressful as attending your first bar mitzvah. There is a certain set of rules that bring order and eliminate chaos. For example, who would know growing up Lutheran in South Dakota that you don't have to bring presents to a bar mitzvah? So as a novice attendee of sporting events, you will not want to make any glaring public errors while trying to impress somebody that you are a sports kind of person.

Let's start at the beginning. You're in the office and somebody says, "I've got two tickets to the Knicks game tonight, anybody in?" Social lesson number one: You're not in because anybody who has two tickets to a Knicks game and hasn't been able to find a partner is in some kind of social trouble himself. Or, more likely, his tickets suck. So stay away from that one. Then again, if somebody comes up and says, "Say, I've got two tickets to the Knicks game next Friday. I think you'd like it." Now you're talking. So suddenly you're going to a Knicks game.

(Note: I don't mean to eliminate all the other teams. And I really don't mean to go Eastern on you here. Going Eastern in my business means the following: You are sitting in front of your television watching a sporting event and sportscasters always refer to events in Eastern Time. This is what bothers those of us who live in California: Sportscasters in the East always say "good night" when it's daytime in the West. So when it's four o'clock in the afternoon and the sun is at a 75-degree angle and Chris Berman or Bob Costas or I say, "Good night, everybody," we have gone Eastern on you, and we apologize.

Then again, when you are in a New York studio and it's seven o'clock and you're finally done reading numbers all day, you're not really thinking about where the surf is up.)

So where were we? Oh yes, the Knicks game. First of all, you want to make sure you are calling where you are going the correct name. Yes, it's the Knicks game. But if Michael Jordan is in town, you refer to it simply as "The Game." If the Clippers are in town, you call it "a night out." But in New York, saying you are going to the Knicks game puts you a couple of notches above your friends. In Los Angeles, saying you are going to a Lakers game brings out similar vibrations in people. Here's a shortcut to talking tickets in New York and Los Angeles:

HE: I've got two tickets to the Knicks/Lakers game tonight.

YOU (beginners level): Who's playing? (You're searching.)

HE: The Celtics.

YOU (looking for *any* crumb of information to keep the conversation going): Who'd they get in the draft, again?

HE: Ron Mercer.

YOU (not knowing who Mercer is): Oh yeah, I haven't seen him since college.

HE: He was great at Kentucky.

And now, if you have your B.S. handbook available, you can dig in and gather up some Kentucky fact. Gather up a couple of old Celtic facts and you're set.

Now let's go through this at an intermediate level:

HE: I've got two tickets to the Knicks/Lakers game tonight.

YOU (knowing the team): Great. I'd like to see how Boston looks.

HE: They are the worst team in the league.

YOU: Well, sure, but Pitino is gonna improve them some, don't you think? And I really want to see how Mercer is coming along.

HE: He was great at Kentucky.

Now at an advanced level:

HE: I've got two tickets to the Knicks/Lakers game tonight.

YOU: Are they floor seats?

OBNOXIOUS TALK

HE: I've got two tickets to the Knicks game tonight.

YOU: I haven't supported the Knicks since Dick Barnett was playing.

So you see, saying the right thing can be crucial. And, by the way, if somebody actually has floor seats, he will say straightaway, "I've got two floor seats to the Knicks game tonight." Floor seats are a big deal. People pay a thousand dollars to sit next to celebrities who don't pay a thousand dollars but are sitting there free because you are paying a thousand dollars.

WHAT TO WEAR

So you're going to a game. What to wear becomes an immediate issue because you are thinking, Well, it *is* a sporting event, so I should dress sporty, right? Not always. If you are going to a Raiders game, tank tops and anything that says Marriott or Pepsi on it will do. A Green Bay Packers game screams for a down sleeping bag. I'm not kidding. The fans at Lambeau Field pour themselves into the bags, pour themselves a beverage, and sit there in the stands in the Arctic weather and enjoy the game.

So you have to pick your spots. The key is not to stick out. You don't want to wear that leather miniskirt with the halter top because you'll be in every television cutaway and up on *SportsCenter*. You'll also want to leave home your multicolored wig and John 3:16 banner. And, just to put you on the next level, stay away from Lakers shirts at a Lakers game and Dodger-wear at a Dodgers game. It's just too, well, sporty. You're going out. You're spending some big bucks here. Make it a good time.

So dress as if you are going to a bar and grill. Nothing fancy, nothing grubby. Even those people who sit in the floor seats can usually be seen with jeans and a sport coat or jeans and a sweater. Celebrity dress-down is a good rule of thumb. Jeans that might be tattered somewhere and a pair of $500 Manolo Blahniks.

Unless you are leaving right after work, coats and ties and good pantsuits are for snobs and Colgate graduates.

WHAT TO BRING

You don't want to be asking your friends what to bring because it is a sure sign you have never been to a game. You don't even want to ask somebody you consider a really good friend something like "Should I bring something to eat?" No. In this day and age, the first thing you want to bring is a lot of money.

Even if you are not paying for the tickets, going to a sporting event in these great economic times means helping out the sporting world economy. Want to know how quickly the money goes?

Program $5, souvenir T-shirt $50, hot dog and beer $10, miscellaneous food $20, miscellaneous souvenirs $100. Multiply the total by the number of people who are going and you've got yourself an "I Helped the Economy" T-Shirt. (Be sure to factor in dry cleaning after the moron behind you spills his Molson all over the new suede jacket that you bought to wear to the game.)

You'll also want to bring a pair of binoculars. The person who has invited you may not have the seats he thought they had, so you may be far enough away to warrant binocs. Even if the seats are *good,* you'll want to people watch. Or count the number of women wearing Manolo Blahnik shoes. Also, if you want to see what the NBA looked like in the 1950s, turn the binoculars around and you'll see a bunch of little guys running around the floor.

What *not* to bring: A flask. A banner of any kind. A sign that says something like "Hey, Mom, Send Money," or "Michael Rules," or any combination of ABC, CBS, or NBC, such as "Atlanta Beats Celtics," "Celtics Beat Seattle," "Nobody But Carillo." Doesn't work.

Do *not* bring any noisemakers. No whistles. Stay away from those big foam number one fingers. No TVs. Nothing worse than somebody who is at a live event watching television. Radios only if you are at a game being called by Ernie Harwell or Vin Scully or Chick Hearn. No sunglasses indoors, unless you are so cool that the sun always shines.

WHAT TO DO WHEN YOU GET IN

This is easy. Just act confident. Remember when your mom and dad used to say, "Act as if you've been there before"? Well, don't wander around for 45 minutes looking for your seats. Ask an usher. Even regulars ask ushers. Don't put your head in a locked-up position staring at the banners on the ceiling. Don't continue to say, "Far out, this is wild." No, no, no. Just casually walk to your seat and slyly look around and sit down. If the game's going on, calmly look at the score. If the numbers are close, it's a close game. You say: "Great. Good game so far." Then shut up. Cheer when your partner cheers, watch out for that guy behind you, and go spend that money.

DURING THE GAME

Even if you have no idea what's going on—and if you are reading this, there's a good chance you don't—smile and pretend to enjoy yourself. If you don't know the nuances of the game you are supposed to be enjoying, focus on something. Sometimes it's just as much fun to watch a game away from the ball. Pick a couple of tackles and watch them run around. Watch that player who never gets the ball and who is setting a pick. Watch an outfielder talk with the fans, or, in the case of Albert Belle, catch batteries and foreign objects from the fans.

Being at a game is pretty much the same as watching at home, except the concessions are more expensive.

AFTER THE GAME

Congratulations, you made it all the way (we hope) through your first game. It's not a good thing to be seen leaving early. It is, in fact, slightly un-American.

Game's over. Win or lose, you've enjoyed the experience. Sometime during the game, check the schedule so that on your way out you can refer to the next game or series, as in "They won't be able to do that against the Cowboys next Sunday." Or "Try that one against the big guy in Houston."

Memorize the score. You'll be big-time the next day when someone asks you, "How was the game?" You'll beam as you report: "One-point game," or "Twenty-point blowout."

And even if you still can't remember Mike Piazza's name, do remember that he hit a home run, and then go look for his name in the newspaper. Talk sports all day at the office. Even mentioning that hot dog puts you in the major leagues.

You were there. You did it. You're a sports fan. You're clueless. But most people are.

Welcome to March. Make no mistake about it, this is the month of college basketball. Period. Much like January, when everyone thinks he is an expert on professional football—especially around Super Bowl Sunday— in late March, everybody *is* an expert on college hoops. This is because March Madness—the name given the hoopla surrounding the NCAA Tournament—is the kind of event probably even you have followed. And why are you and everybody else an expert? Because in March we all go back to college, we all find somebody to root for, we all fill out those brackets, and we all pretend we picked the winners. This culminates in what is called the Final Four, arguably the greatest day in sports. This is on a Saturday, and the championship game to decide the college national champs, is on the following Monday.

The madness begins about the second week in March, when there is what they call "Selection Sunday." This is the day 64 college basketball teams—out of roughly 300—are chosen to play in the tournament. Before Selection Sunday, you should be telling friends how excited you are that the tournament is finally around the corner and you are wondering who will be the number one seeds in each region.

The country is divided into four regions—the Midwest, the West, the Southeast, and the East. This can change from year to year, but the general idea is that teams are sent to distinctly different parts of the United States. You will wonder where the top teams will go. Think in fours, since at the end of the tourney, which is called the "Final Four," you will want to look at the top four teams in college basketball just before Se-lection Sunday. If, say, Duke is number one, you'll wonder if it will get to play near home or if "it will be sent out west." You can recall how UCLA on a number of occasions has been sent away from its home base and it's been a disaster. But to make it simple, take the top four teams and start guessing along with everybody else where they'll go.

Coming up to Selection Sunday, you'll hear terms like "on the bubble," which means a team may or not make the tourna-ment, and "top seed," which means a team will get early first-round games. This is also called a "high seed." A "low seed" refers to a team that "got off the bubble" and made it into the tournament and thus may have to play a high seed early. For example, you don't want to play Duke in the first round of a lose-and-out tournament. Or North Carolina or Kansas or who-ever is in the top echelon at the time. Get it? Don't worry. In March, it's pounded into you by everybody around you. Just smile and keep saying, "They gotta win six." That's how many games you have to win to win it all. So anytime something hap-pens and somebody wonders if his team got into the wrong re-gion or got a tough road to the Final Four, you say: "You gotta win six."

Another thing you can always look for is "returning starters." You won't sound dumb if you ask somebody, "How many returning starters does he have?" He won't know either and will probably lie, so you get points here. You can have an entire tournament conversation by talking only about injuries. Just keep saying "if they are healthy." And always finish with "you gotta win six."

Coaching matchups are always good conversation. Al-ways go with coaches you've heard of, because if you've heard of them, they've been in the news: Mike Krzyzewski of Duke,

Bob Knight of Indiana, John Thompson of Georgetown, Roy Williams of Kansas. With each of these guys you can always say, "I wouldn't want to face Mike Krzyzewski" or "How would you like to go up against John Thompson in the second round?" Or "Is there a better big-game coach than Bob Knight?" It's good stuff. Be sure to say Krzyzewski correctly. It's Sha-CHEF-ski. Or, in a pinch, it's Coach K.

As you get into the flow of the tournament, have fun with it. The bottom line is that there are so many games and so many players and so many coaches and so many different kinds of situations that virtually everybody is so confused that most of the so-called experts wait until the Final Four to start talking it up really big. In the meantime, put these key tournament moments in your pocket and maybe by April we'll be calling *you* "coach."

MARCH 17, 1939

The first NCAA Tournament got under way in Philadelphia as Villanova beat Brown by 12 and Ohio State defeated Wake Forest, also by 12.

MARCH 21, 1964

UCLA defeated Duke, 98–83, giving John Wooden and UCLA the first of ten national titles. UCLA, starting no one taller than 6'5", utilized a full-court zone press that maximized the team's quickness. Gail Goodrich had 27 points for the winners. Including the 1964 tournament, UCLA would go on to win 38 consecutive tournament games, a streak that would last until 1974, when David Thompson and North Carolina State beat the Bruins in two overtimes in the national semifinals at the Final Four. Remember, UCLA's 88-game win streak also ended in 1974 at Notre Dame.

MARCH 11, 1985

The first annual Bob Knight chair-throwing contest was held. The event came about after the hot-tempered Indiana basketball coach's outburst during a game against Purdue the previous month when he threw a chair in anger.

MARCH 19, 1966

Texas Western (now the University of Texas at El Paso), fielding a predominantly black squad coached by Don Haskins, recorded a historical win over Adolph Rupp and Kentucky. Pat Riley had 19 points in a losing effort for the Wildcats. The final score was 72–65. Bobby Joe Hill led the Texans with 20 points. In the wake of Texas Western's great performance, major Southern schools started altering their unwritten directives by recruiting more African-American players.

MARCH 23, 1957

North Carolina, coached by New York City native Frank McGuire, beat Kansas and Wilt Chamberlain in triple overtime to win the NCAA title and cap a perfect 32–0 season. The Tar Heels had defeated Michigan State in three overtimes to advance to the title game. UNC was led by starter Lennie Rosenbluth, who was born in the Bronx and went to Carolina largely because of McGuire's ties to the Big Apple.

UNC beat Kansas 54–53 and defeated Michigan State by a score of 74–70. Rosenbluth averaged 25.5 points per game in the two wins. McGuire sent 5'11" Tommy Kearns out to jump the opening tip versus Wilt Chamberlain. Chamberlain was over seven feet tall! Of course, Chamberlain won the tip, but the Heels won the game. Chamberlain had 23 points and 14 rebounds in the loss.

MARCH 27, 1939

Oregon, coached by Howard Hobson, defeated Ohio State 46–33 to win the first-ever NCAA Tournament. Nicknamed "Tall Firs," Oregon started four native Oregonians and one Washingtonian. Just eight schools participated in the inaugural tournament. Oregon was nicknamed the Tall Firs because it had more size than most schools: a 6'8" center and a pair of 6'4" forwards. John Dick's 13 points took scoring honors. Dick would go on to serve as an admiral in the U.S. Navy, commanded the aircraft carrier *Saratoga* for two years, and served as chief of staff for all carrier forces in the Western Pacific.

MARCH 28, 1992

In the East Regional championship, Duke shocked Kentucky, 104–103, in overtime as Christian Laettner grabbed teammate Grant Hill's full-court pass, turned, and hit a jumper to put the Blue Devils into the Final Four. Laettner was 10–10 from the field and 10–10 from the line in a 31-point performance. Duke went on to beat Michigan in the national title game nine days later. The Blue Devils still remain the only team since UCLA in 1974 to repeat as national champions. Duke beat Kansas the year before to give Coach K his first national title in his fifth Final Four appearance.

___

MARCH 31, 1997

Arizona, a fourth seed, beat Kentucky 84–79 in overtime to win the school's first basketball national championship. The Wildcats scored all ten of their overtime points from the free-throw line.

They beat Kansas, North Carolina, and Kentucky, three of college basketball's schools with the highest win percentage, in a span of 11 days. Arizona became the first-ever school to beat three number one seeds in one tournament!

The Wildcats had lost four of their last eight games entering the tournament. Miles Simon, Darryl Strawberry's brother-in-law, was named Most Outstanding Player of the Final Four.

___

**In March, college basketball month,
one of basketball's greatest nights unfolded.**

MARCH 2, 1962

Wilt Chamberlain of the Philadelphia Warriors scored 100 points in an NBA game against the New York Knicks in Hershey, Pennsylvania. Chamberlain was 36 for 63 from the field and 28 for 32 from the free-throw line. He also grabbed 25 rebounds in that game. The Warriors beat the Knicks, 169–147. Philadelphia's second-leading scorer, guard Al Attles, had 17 points, including eight for eight from the field. Chamberlain scored 31 points in the fourth period to reach 100 and shot 88 percent from the line that night. He ended his career as a 51 percent free-throw shooter. Think of how many *more* points he could have had in his career if he had been a good free-throw shooter. He holds the NBA career record for free-throw attempts with 11,862. Wilt played in 1,205 total games (regular season and play-offs) without fouling out of a contest. In Wilt's 100-point game, New York scored 147 points with three players scoring over 30 points apiece and the Knicks still fell by 22! Only 4,124 witnessed the historic occasion. Wilt had 98 points with 1:27 left, but missed three shots. With 46 seconds left, Joe Ruklick hit Wilt with a pass, and he hit a short shot.

The time to use this story is whenever somebody is having a big scoring night. If you want to be cute, you can ask anybody which two players combined for 117 points in an NBA game. The answer is, of course, Al Attles and Wilt Chamberlain. Al once told me, "I would have had more points, but I couldn't get the ball away from Wilt." I've always kidded Wilt that since there is no definitive *video* of the game—only still pictures— that it really didn't happen. Anybody can take a still picture of a guy holding a sign up with the number 100 on it. But believe me, it did happen.

Important note: Anytime somebody starts telling you that Dennis Rodman is the greatest rebounder of all time, throw out this: Wilt *averaged* 22.9 rebounds in his career. Dennis averages 18.7. (Always put those tenths in. They sound good. Never round off stats.) Wilt led the league in rebounding 11 times. He once had 55 rebounds in *one* game. Twice he had 45 in a game. It's safe to say he owns the record books in this category. There were other categories Wilt said he owned— like his claim he was "with" 20,000 women—but we're not going there. You can, but don't do it around Wilt.

We said that Wilt never fouled out of a game.

MARCH 12, 1956

Wilt Chamberlain played 1,205 total games in his NBA career, and *never* fouled out of a contest. Syracuse's Dick Farley set an NBA record by fouling out in five minutes against St. Louis. Farley fouled out of seven games in his 233-game career.

March is a prelude to baseball, the sport we get ready for the minute the final out is called in the World Series. So it's always good to have a couple of good baseball stories to pepper your conversations with. For example, on March 5, 1973, New York Yankee pitchers Mike Kekich and Fritz Peterson announced the strangest trade in baseball history when they admitted that they swapped *wives* during the off season. They also traded their families to each other. Perhaps it is no surprise that Kekich and Peterson were left-handed pitchers. Peterson eventually married Suzanne Kekich, while the relationship between Kekich and Marilyn Peterson did not last.

MARCH 1, 1969

New York Yankee great Mickey Mantle announced his retirement from baseball. Mantle, from Commerce, Oklahoma, was dubbed "The Commerce Comet." Primarily a center fielder, Mantle replaced Joe DiMaggio at that position. Mantle was named Mickey after baseball great Mickey Cochrane. A powerful switch-hitter, Mantle was a three-time

MVP and a 1974 inductee into baseball's Hall of Fame. He and teammate Roger Maris became known as the "M and M boys." Mantle holds a slew of World Series records. He finished his Yankee career with 536 home runs and gave baseball fans across the nation many thrills.

MARCH 13, 1954

Milwaukee Braves outfielder Bobby Thomson fractured his ankle in spring training and was replaced by a rookie named Henry Aaron. Three years earlier, Thomson had changed his position to open up a spot for rookie Willie Mays when both played for the New York Giants. Thomson's greatest feat was hitting the "shot heard 'round the world," a three-run homer off Brooklyn right-hander Ralph Branca that capped the Giants' historic comeback to win the National League pennant in 1951. The Dodgers led 4–1 going into the bottom of the ninth, but Thomson's shot won the game and the three-game postseason play-off. Russ Hodges's call of "The Giants win the pennant" after Thomson's homer is well known. The Giants went on to lose the '51 World Series in six games to the New York Yankees and Casey Stengel.

Let everybody talk about Mickey Mantle all they want. He's a legend, for sure. He was the guy every kid wanted to be growing up in the fifties and sixties. But consider this: In his regular-season career, he struck out and walked a combined 3,444 times. Divide this by an average number of at-bats in a season and that comes out to about seven seasons without putting the bat on the ball. You say: "Did you know Mantle didn't hit the ball for seven full seasons?" People will gasp. You'll throw this heat at them and you've struck them out.

**When you talk about superstars, sometimes
you can include a broadcaster. Not many,
mind you. Last month we talked about the
late Red Barber and Mel Allen. This month:
Chick Hearn. You can also throw this one in
at the office when somebody either has
never called in sick or is away more than
Johnny Carson was in the summertime.**

MARCH 13, 1992

Francis Dayle Hearn, better known as "Chick" Hearn, broadcast his consecutive game number 2,500 as L.A. Lakers announcer in a game at Cleveland. Hearn got his nickname because when he was an AAU basketball player he was handed a box of sneakers and was surprised to find a chicken inside! In the fall of 1986 a star with his name was installed on Hollywood Boulevard's Walk of Fame. Hearn has not missed a game since November 20, 1965. He has announced the games of Jerry West and Elgin Baylor, Wilt Chamberlain, Kareem Abdul-Jabbar, Magic Johnson, and Shaquille O'Neal.

March is also the month of the Iditarod. And it's not the Iditarod Dog Sled race . . . it's the Iditarod Sled Dog race. A time when men are men, dogs are dogs, women are women, and nobody can understand why these people are doing this. I've covered three Iditarods, and while I can report that the dogs eat better than the drivers, other than that, it is truly a test of will and skill. I was there when Libby Riddles won it for the first time. The first *woman* to win the thing and you would have thought Tiger Woods had won the Masters. What follows are the only Iditarod stories you'll need for now.

MARCH 3, 1973

❄️Thirty-six men and their dog teams competed in the first Iditarod from Anchorage to Nome. Twenty days later, Dick Wilmarth of Red Devil, Alaska, crossed the finish line on Front Street in Nome. Wilmarth won the $12,000 prize by completing the 1,100-mile course in officially 20 days, 0 hours, 49 minutes, and 41 seconds. "Iditarod" is a Shageluk Indian word meaning "clear water" used as the name of the Iditarod River. Another source claims it's an Ingalik Indian word, "haiditarod," meaning "distant place." With a couple of past exceptions, the race always begins on the first Saturday in March. Wilmarth won the first race, but he never entered again. The race crosses two mountain ranges, two great rivers, and the sea of ice of Norton Sound. The official name is the Iditarod Trail Sled Dog Race. It's billed as the "last great race on Earth."

In the first race, last-place finisher John Schultz finished nearly two weeks behind Wilmarth. Schultz won the initial *Red Lantern,* awarded to the final finisher each year. Why a red lantern? It's more or less a statement that those who passed that way before will leave a light burning for you.

The highest point on the Iditarod Trail is Rainy Pass at an elevation of 3,160 feet.

In 1974, Mary Shields of College, Alaska, was the first woman to complete the Iditarod Trail Race with her lead dog, Cabbage. Libby Riddles, from Teller, Alaska, was the first-ever women's winner, in 1985. Led by her lead dog, Granite, Susan Butcher won the 1986, '87, '88, and '90 races. When Butcher visited President Bush in April 1990, she brought Granite along!

Rick Swenson has won five Iditarods (1977, '79, '81, '82, and '91), more than anyone else.

"Mush!," "Hike!," "All right," and "Let's go!" are all commands to start the team.

The lead dog, or leader, is the dog who runs in front of the others. Generally, the dog must be both intelligent and fast.

Hockey. As long as it's cold, it's always good to have a hockey story to unfold for your friends. And you might as well just stick with the two great ones.

MARCH 23, 1994

Wayne Gretzky, then of the L.A. Kings, scores goal number 802 versus Vancouver and net minder Kirk McLean. This goal broke Gordie Howe's NHL career regular-season goals-scored record. Howe scored his 801 goals for Detroit and Hartford over a 26-year NHL career. Gretzky made his debut on October 10, 1979, with Edmonton. Four days later, he scored his first career goal against goaltender Glen Hanlon of Vancouver. He scored a goal on October 9, 1982, versus Vancouver, becoming the player to rack up 200 career goals in the shortest amount of time. His five hundredth career goal also came against Vancouver.

MARCH 31, 1928

Gordie Howe was born in Floral, Saskatchewan. One of the NHL's greatest-ever players, Howe finally stopped playing hockey in the NHL at age 52. In his final season, with Hartford, Howe played 80 games, scoring 15 goals for the 1979–80 Whalers. Other older professional athletes include Oakland's George Blanda, who, at age 48, kicked thirteen field goals and 44 extra points and completed one of three passes for the '75 Raiders. Blanda holds the NFL record for seasons played at 26 and most career points with 2,002. The breakdown is as follows: 943 PATs, 335 field goals, and 9 touchdowns. Blanda was (and is) the only player to celebrate a silver anniversary in pro football. Baseball's Hoyt Wilhelm, born in 1923, pitched in 16 games for the 1972 L.A. Dodgers.

MARCH 5, 1984

Brigham Young University quarterback Steve Young signed a long-term contract with the L.A. Express of the USFL. Young played two seasons in the USFL, throwing 16 touchdown passes and running for 9 touchdowns. After being released by the Express on September 9, 1985, Young went to Tampa Bay in the NFL for two seasons. He was then traded to the 49ers from the Bucs for a second- and fourth-round pick in the 1987 draft and cash.

MARCH 7, 1954

The Minneapolis Lakers hosted the Milwaukee Hawks in an NBA game played with 12-foot-high baskets. The game, watched by many league officials, was an experiment to slow down 6'10½" George Mikan and his Minneapolis teammate, 6'9" Clyde Lovellette. The 12-foot baskets were used just for this game.

MARCH 8, 1971

Joe Frazier won a 15-round decision over Muhammad Ali in their long-awaited bout. The fight was close until the fifteenth round, when a Frazier left hook floored Ali. The fight, one of the most lucrative sports events in history, grossed nearly $20,000,000, mostly through receipts from closed-circuit television. Ali's loss ended his winning streak after 31 triumphs, including 25 knockouts.

MARCH 19, 1969

NBA commissioner J. Walter Kennedy flipped a coin, Phoenix called "heads," and it came up "tails." Milwaukee got the first pick in the 1969 NBA draft, taking UCLA center Kareem Abdul-Jabbar (known then as Lew Alcindor). Phoenix took Florida's Neal Walk with the number two pick. Abdul-Jabbar went on to six NBA titles and an NBA career record of 38,387 points. Walk finished his eight-year pro career with 7,157 points.

MARCH 13, 1983

Randy Smith of the San Diego Clippers played the final game in his NBA record consecutive-games-played-streak, against Dallas. The streak lasted 906 games and began on February 18, 1972, when Smith was playing for Buffalo. A. C. Green broke this streak in 1997.

MARCH 18, 1972

Carolina's Larry Miller scored 67 points in a game against Memphis to set an ABA record for points in a game. Miller averaged 28.4 points for the 1971–72 season. Some fellow named Julius Erving finished the season sixth in the ABA in scoring, averaging 27.3 points per game for the Virginia Squires. Erving was a rookie in 1971–72, but Kentucky's Artis Gilmore beat him out for Rookie of the Year honors. Gilmore was also selected as MVP. Erving would lead the ABA in scoring in his second and third seasons in the now defunct league.

MARCH 20, 1984

Indiana's Butch Carter scored 14 points in an overtime period against the Celtics, setting an NBA record for most points in an overtime period. Indiana won the game, 123–121. Carter averaged 13.4 points a game that season. Trivia note: Carter is the brother of Vikings superstar wideout Cris Carter of the NFL.

MARCH 21, 1953

Boston defeated Syracuse, 111–105, in four overtimes as an NBA play-off record 106 personal fouls were rung up for both teams combined. Seven Syracuse and five Boston players fouled out of the game.

MARCH 23, 1952

Right winger Bill Mosienko of the Chicago Black Hawks recorded the fastest hat trick in NHL history. He scored three goals in just 21 seconds against New York Rangers goaltender Lorne Anderson in the third period. All three goals were with both teams at full strength. Chicago won the game, 7–6.

In the month of April nothing major has ever happened in professional or college sports. April Fool. The fact is, as you'll soon be able to point out, April has traditionally given us some of the greatest moments in sports. Be it the NCAA championship basketball game or Tiger Woods walking up 18 at Augusta, or baseball Opening Day fanfare, April is a breath of the fresh air it produces.

Since this is a month when lots of sporting events crunch up next to each other, when you are out B.S.-ing about sports, you'll have a variety of subjects to go to.

You know, one of the key tricks to talking sports is your ability to get the conversation to where *you* want it, to where *your* heavy base of information is. You'll notice that even the people you think are the best at talking sports are seriously limited. They always get the conversation back to the same anecdote. The same superstar. The same big inning. But with the following grab bag you can overcome the risk of becoming a "sports bore." You will be "sports versatile." So go ahead and pick your topic.

**Basketball: Begin on April Fools' Day
with one of the greatest upsets in sports.
Brent Musburger fired from CBS? No . . .**

APRIL 1, 1985

Eighth-seed Villanova shocked mighty Georgetown, 66–61, to win the NCAA Tournament. The Wildcats shot 78.6 percent (22 of 28) from the field to knock off the Hoyas. Reserve guard Harold Jensen came off the bench to score 14 points on 5 of 5 shooting. The Wildcats' patient and methodical offense frustrated the more talented Hoyas. Georgetown had 25 more shot attempts, but still lost. 'Nova was 22 of 27 from the free-throw line to Georgetown's 6 of 8. That was the difference. The 1985 Final Four featured three Big East teams (Villanova, Georgetown, St. John's) and Memphis State (now Memphis).

The Villanova upset is your key upset game. Anybody can predict an upset and anybody will, but you want an *improbable* upset and that was it. Unless you consider April 4, 1983, when sixth-seed North Carolina State and coach Jim Valvano knocked off Houston, 54–52, in Albuquerque, New Mexico, to win the school's second-ever national championship. The Wolfpack also won it in 1974 behind David Thompson. In '83, they won it all on the strength of Lorenzo Charles's last-second basket. With the score tied at 52, senior guard Derek Whittenburg launched a desperation 30-footer that fell just short of the rim. Charles grabbed the ball out of the air and dunked it home with two ticks left to win the game. Despite having ten losses, Valvano's team knocked off Hakeem Olajuwon, Clyde Drexler, and the rest of the top-ranked and heavily favored Houston Cougars.

How about a woman-in-sports story? Try this one around a gang of cigar-smoking macho men who think they know everything. They'll envy you.

APRIL 4, 1993

Texas Tech's Sheryl Swoopes broke Bill Walton's points record in a Division I title game by putting up 47 against Ohio State in the national championship game at the Omni in Atlanta. Swoopes, who played just two years of major-college basketball, scored 1,645 points and had a 24.9 average. She came to Texas Tech from South Plains Junior College in Texas, where she held 28 school records. At Texas Tech, she shot 54 percent from the field and 84 percent from the free-throw line in two years. She also averaged nine rebounds per game. The '93 Final Four was the first advance sellout since the women embraced a Final Four format in 1978. The Las Vegas bookmakers even put a line on the three games in 1993.

The first woman to bring showtime to college basketball was Nancy Lieberman, who captained two national title teams at Old Dominion in Norfolk, Virginia, and was a three-time Kodak all-American. In 1976, as an 18-year-old graduate of a Far Rockaway, New York, high school, she played on the '76 silver medal team in the Olympics. She was nicknamed "Lady Magic" because of her fancy passing ability.

In April 1896, the first known women's intercollegiate varsity game was played. Stanford defeated Cal 2–1 after playing two 20-minute halves.

**When you see a turnover, go ahead
and tell the guys about the greatest one ever.**

APRIL 15, 1965

With Philadelphia trailing Boston 110–109 at Boston Garden, Celtic John Havlicek deflected an in-bounds pass by
Philly's Hal Greer to preserve the Eastern Division Finals Game
7. Celtics announcer Johnny Most had the call: "Havlicek stole
the ball! Havlicek stole the ball!" Boston went on to win its seventh consecutive NBA title that year. The Celts beat the Lakers
in five games. Note the early date for a division finals Game 7.
Now, the contest would be in May.

**From 1997 on, April will be known as the
month Tiger Woods won the Masters. It
was one of the greatest moments in
sports. Tie it in with Jackie Robinson and
you've got an evening of electric conversation.**

APRIL 13, 1997

Tiger Woods, 21, who is of African-American and Thai
heritage, became the youngest golfer in history to win
the Masters at the Augusta National Golf Club. Woods's final
round of 69 on this day gave him a total score of an 18-under-
par 270, the lowest in the 61-year history of the event. That's a
270 over 72 holes. His 12-stroke win was the biggest margin
of victory ever at Augusta.

According to an April 1997 report in *The Boston Globe*,
four-year-old Robert Aldred from Warley, England, can drive a

golf ball 140 yards and par 345-yard holes. He started at 18 months with a plastic driver and golf balls.

APRIL 15, 1947

Major-league baseball's first black player in this century, Jackie Robinson, went hitless in three at-bats against Boston in his debut. Robinson, batting second and playing first base for the Brooklyn Dodgers in his first game, went on to win National League Rookie of the Year honors. He batted .297 with 12 homers and 29 stolen bases his rookie season. The first major-league pitcher Robinson faced was the Braves' Johnny Sain. Robinson won the National League MVP in 1949, led the league in steals in '47 and '49, and won the league's batting title in '49 with a .342 average. Robinson was a great athlete at UCLA, excelling in football, basketball, and track along with his baseball exploits. Utilizing that speed and quickness, Robinson stole home 19 times in his 10-year major-league career. He retired after the 1956 season. He was elected into baseball's Hall of Fame in 1962. He died on October 24, 1972, at age fifty-three.

Oh, somebody will always bring up Greg Norman and call him a choker. You're going to be smart and never call any athlete a choker, especially not somebody who makes as much money as Greg and somebody who, while giving the leader of the Western world golf tips, ends up putting the president in a cast.

APRIL 14, 1996

Greg Norman blew a huge lead at the Masters in Augusta, Georgia. Through three rounds, Norman's 63-69-71 = 203 put him at 13 under par, six shots ahead of Nick Faldo. Norman shot a 78 on the final round. Faldo? A 67. It was Faldo's third green jacket win. He's come from three, five, and six shots behind on the last day to win!

Hard-line golfers will never let go of Jack Nicklaus. Don't let them.

APRIL 13, 1986

Forty-six-year-old Jack Nicklaus shot a final-round 65 to win his sixth Masters. Nicklaus hadn't won a PGA event in two years before the win. In fact, his highest showing in '86 before the win was thirty-ninth place at the Hawaiian Open. In 1986, Nicklaus landed a 74 and a 71 in his first two rounds earlier in the week. Forget the Golden Bear, he was the Olden Bear!

Having a bad day in April? Is it your boss? Tell him or her about Lou Gehrig's and Babe Ruth's nightmare days. Getting up- staged by a teenager. And a girl at that.

APRIL 2, 1931

Jackie Mitchell, age 17, struck out Lou Gehrig *and* Babe Ruth in an exhibition game in Chattanooga, Tennessee, when she pitched against the Yankees. After striking out Ruth and Gehrig, she walked Tony Lazzeri and then was taken out of the game by manager Bert Niehoff.

In the 1934 All-Star Game, southpaw Carl Hubbell of the New York Giants consecutively struck out Babe Ruth, Lou Gehrig, Jimmie Foxx, Al Simmons, and Joe Cronin in the first and second innings. Hubbell and his five strikeout victims were all inducted into the Baseball Hall of Fame. In fact, 17 of the 18 starters in that All-Star Game were eventually elected to the Hall. The odd man out? Boston Braves slugger Wally Berger. That game was truly an "All-Star" affair. In 1986, L.A. Dodgers hurler Fernando Valenzuela fanned Don Mattingly, Cal Ripken, Jr., Jesse Barfield, Lou Whitaker, and pitcher Ted Higuera in succession! Both Hubbell and Valenzuela depended on the screwball as their number one pitch.

When talkin' sports, inevitably you'll run into the long argument over the DH, the designated hitter. This argument always becomes passionate at the least and furious at the worst. Memorize this and the purists will vote you into their hall of fame.

APRIL 6, 1973

Ron Blomberg of the New York Yankees made history by becoming the first player in the annals of major-league baseball ever to bat as a designated hitter. A good hit, no field player with the Yankees, this day he went one for three against Boston's Luis Tiant. Blomberg quipped about the term "DH": "I've been a DH all my life: designated Hebrew."

April—except in strike years—gives us Opening
Day in major-league baseball. This is a hallowed
occasion. People cut work. People cut school. People
lie to get out of business trips. All to get to an
Opening Day game. If they don't go, they sometimes
will tell you they went. Someone, some day, is going
to invite you to an Opening Day. Dress up
(preferably warmly). Leave your cell phone at
home. Don't eat, you'll be eating hot dogs at the old
ball yard. Bring a camera for your Opening Day
photo with a bunch of strangers. Cry during the
national anthem. Boo the opposing team. Try to stay
for the entire game. During the game tell any one
of these stories. They'll love you in the box seats
and adore you in the bleachers.

APRIL 7, 1979

Houston Astros pitcher Ken Forsch threw a no-hitter
against the Atlanta Braves, duplicating his younger
brother Bob's feat from the year before. Bob no-hit the Phillies
on April 16, 1978, when he was a member of the St. Louis Cardinals. Bob, a converted third baseman, threw a second no-
hitter in 1983 versus Montreal. Bob finished his Cardinals
career with 163 wins. Only Bob Gibson and Jesse Haines won
more in a Cardinals uniform. Bob was also a solid-hitting
pitcher, clubbing 12 home runs in his 16-year career.

APRIL 8, 1974

Atlanta Braves slugger Hank Aaron hits career home run number 715 off L.A. Dodgers pitcher Al Downing to break Babe Ruth's record for career homers in the major leagues. Aaron completed his 23-year major-league career in Milwaukee in 1976 with 755 lifetime homers. He was elected to baseball's Hall of Fame in 1982. Some trivia about Aaron includes his *never* hitting 50 homers in a single season. Forty-seven, in 1971, was number 44's career-high. Braves reliever Tom House got his 15 minutes of fame when Aaron hit the record breaker by catching the ball in the Braves bull pen. Hammerin' Hank is the first player listed in *The Baseball Encyclopedia*. His late brother, Tommie, also played with the Atlanta Braves, from 1968 to 1971. Tommie also played with the Milwaukee Braves from 1962 to 1965. He hit 13 career home runs, 742 behind his older brother. The Aaron brothers were born in Mobile, Alabama. Other baseball standouts born in Mobile include Satchel Paige, Willie McCovey, and Amos Otis. Also, Al Downing and Hank Aaron were both wearing jersey number 44 that night.

APRIL 18, 1981

The Pawtucket Pawsox of the AAA International League hosted the Rochester Red Wings. The game began around 8 P.M. At 4:07 A.M. play was suspended with the score tied 2–2 after 32 innings. There were 27 fans left at McCoy Stadium. The game was resumed on June 23, and, because of a major-league strike, the entire baseball world was focused on its resumption. Rochester failed to score in the top of the thirty-third, and the Pawsox won it in the home half when Dave

Koza knocked in Marty Barrett. The final tally of the game played on April 18–19 and June 23 was 33 innings, 8 hours, and 25 minutes. Bob Ojeda was the winning pitcher, and Steve Grilli got tagged with the loss. Pawtucket's Wade Boggs won the International League batting title in '81. Teammate Bob Ojeda won the league's ERA title. Cal Ripken, Jr., of Rochester was named Rookie of the Year that season. Boggs and Ripken went a combined 6 for 25 in the game.

APRIL 23, 1952

Knuckleballing relief pitcher Hoyt Wilhelm hit a home run off Boston's Dick Hoover in his first major-league at-bat. Wilhelm, as a member of the New York Giants, tripled in his second career at-bat. He would bat 430 more times in his 21-year big-league career and never hit another home run or triple. Wilhelm began his major-league career as a 28-year-old rookie. The first-ever career reliever to be selected to the Hall of Fame, Wilhelm still holds the record for most pitching appearances with 1,070. He started just 52 games, yet he threw a no-hitter for Baltimore against the Yankees in 1958. It was Baltimore's first-ever no-hitter and occurred on Wilhelm's wedding anniversary. Wilhelm led the National League in ERA as a rookie in 1952 and the American League in 1959.

APRIL 23, 1954

Hank Aaron hit the first of his 755 home runs off St. Louis's Vic Raschi. Don Drysdale allowed 17 of Aaron's 755, the most by any pitcher.

APRIL 23, 1921

Warren Spahn was born. Spahn owns the major-league record for career wins as a left-hander with 363. Spahn hit 35 career homers. He also gave up Willie Mays's first career homer, on May 28, 1951. He allowed more home runs to Mays (18) than any other pitcher.

APRIL 29, 1988

The Baltimore Orioles beat the Chicago White Sox 9–0 to snap an 0 for 21 start to their season. The O's ended up 22½ games behind sixth-place Cleveland. They were 0 for 44 in games in which they scored one run or no runs that season. Only three pitchers were with the team from the season's start to its finish. Sitting in the stands was O's general manager Roland Hemond, wearing the same suit he'd worn when he was general manager of the White Sox the day in 1983 that Chicago clinched the American League West Division Title. Mark Williamson, making just his third big-league start, was Baltimore's winning pitcher in 1988. Jack McDowell was the loser. Eddie Murray homered, and Cal Ripken, Jr., went four for five. After the win, the O's were still 15 games out of first place and it was still just April! Cal's dad, Cal Sr., was the manager for the first six games of the losing streak. Frank Robinson replaced him. Robby then went 0 for 15 before beating Chicago.

APRIL 29, 1986

Boston Red Sox pitcher Roger Clemens whiffed 20 Seattle Mariners en route to setting a major-league baseball record for K's in a nine-inning game. Steve Carlton, Tom Seaver, and Nolan Ryan had previously struck out 19 in a game. The "Rocket Man" struck out the side in three innings and fanned eight straight batters at one point. He walked no one. Oh, by the way: Boston won 3–1 before 13,414 at Fenway Park. Lightning does, in fact, strike twice: On September 18, 1996 (ten years later), Clemens struck out 20 Detroit Tigers, walking no one. Before 8,779 at Tiger Stadium, Clemens also took five other hitters to two strikes. He struck out every Detroit starter, including shortstop Travis Fryman, who got the "Golden Sombrero," whiffing four times. Boston won 4–0.

Remember, or try to convince your friends, that hockey is a sport, too. Here are some April on Ice nuggets.

APRIL 25, 1993

Two-time defending Stanley Cup champion Pittsburgh and its star Mario Lemieux had its NHL record 14-game play-off win streak snapped when New Jersey beat the Penguins, 4–1. Certainly not UCLA's 88-game win streak, but impressive nonetheless.

APRIL 23, 1997

Wayne Gretzky extended his NHL record of play-off hat tricks to nine as the New York Rangers beat Florida, 3–2. Gretzky's nine hat tricks break down to seven three-goal games and two four-goal games. Maurice Richard and Jari Kurri are second with seven career hat tricks in play-off action. Gretzky and Kurri played together with Edmonton in the 1980s. Gretzky scored all three goals against the Panthers in a span of 6:23 in the second period.

APRIL 18, 1987

Pat Lafontaine of the New York Islanders scored the dramatic game-winning goal at 8:42 of the fourth overtime period, giving New York a 3–2 win over the Washington Capitals and a four-game to three series win in the division semifinals. The Caps were up three games to one over the Islanders before their collapse. It was the fifth-longest overtime game in NHL play-off history at the time. This "Easter Epic" ended at 1:56 A.M. on Easter Sunday.

APRIL 4, 1982

In 80 games, Edmonton's Wayne Gretzky scored 212 points, 48 points higher than his own NHL record. In his first three seasons, the Oilers center won three MVP awards. He would go on to win five more in a row. In that magical '81–'82 season, the "Great One" scored 92 goals and tallied 120 assists. He had set the previous record of 164 points in the 1980–81 season. Gretzky played his first season professionally in the WHA. At 17, he signed with the Indianapolis Racers. When they ran out of money after eight games, he was sold to the Oilers. The WHA folded in 1979, and Edmonton entered the NHL. When he was ten years old, he scored 378 goals in 85 games in and around Edmonton.

Don't ever be caught without a marathon story. That can be the downfall of even the greatest sports fan. Nobody has any real marathon stories to tell. I've been involved in my share of sports conversation, and I'll be honest, I've never heard anybody really expound on a marathon, unless they actually competed themselves. So go to the front of the line. Wait for the gun and start talking.

APRIL 21, 1997

The 101st running of the Boston Marathon. Fun facts about the Boston Marathon:

Oldest winner: Clarence DeMar in 1930 at age 41. DeMar won the Marathon seven times, a record.

First Marathon: Fifteen people started, ten finished. John J. McDermott, a lithographer from New York, won in a time of 2 hours, 55 minutes, and 10 seconds in 1897. It was called the Boston Athletic Association Marathon. The distance of the first 26 Boston Marathon was 24 miles, 1,232 yards. Now? It's 26 miles, 385 yards.

Strange footwear: Ronald MacDonald won the 1898 Marathon wearing his bicycle shoes.

Closest finish: 1988, when Kenya's Ibrahim Hussein won by one second over Tanzania's Juma Ikangaa.

John A. Kelley: In 1992, at age 85, ran the last of his 61 Boston Marathons. He won the Marathon in 1935 and 1945.

Women: Not until 1972 did Marathon officials finally agree to recognize females. The first-ever official women's winner was Nina Kuscsik in '72.

Last American winner (male): Greg Meyer of the Greater Boston Track Club, in 1983.

Rosie Ruiz: In 1980, Ruiz jumped into the race unnoticed and took credit for being the first woman finisher. It took a week before the ruse was discovered and the victory was given to Canada's Jacqueline Gareau.

Race start/finish: Starts in Hopkinton and finishes near Copley Square in Boston's Back Bay.

Spectators: About 1 million line the course.

Volunteers in 1997 to help out: About 8,000.

Since 1960s, the race has been run on the third Monday of April.

APRIL 5, 1984

Kareem Abdul-Jabbar broke Wilt Chamberlain's NBA record for regular-season career points, scoring the record breaker against the Utah Jazz in Las Vegas. The basket that surpassed Chamberlain's point total of 31,419 was scored on one of Kareem's patented hook shots. Abdul-Jabbar finished his 20-season NBA career with 38,387 points.

Just 11 days after setting the record, Abdul-Jabbar turned 37 years old. A six-time NBA MVP, Abdul-Jabbar played on six NBA championship teams when he was with Milwaukee and the L.A. Lakers. He also led UCLA to three national titles under

John Wooden. He was elected to the Basketball Hall of Fame in 1995.

APRIL 6, 1987

Sugar Ray Leonard won a split decision over "Marvelous" Marvin Hagler to win the World Boxing Council's middleweight title in Las Vegas and collected an $11 million purse. Leonard was born Ray Charles Leonard on May 17, 1956, in Wilmington, North Carolina. Must be something in the water in Wilmington with Leonard and native son Michael Jordan. His mother named him Ray Charles after the singer, but he was nicknamed Sugar Ray after boxing great Sugar Ray Robinson. Leonard lived up to that billing by winning an Olympic gold medal in 1976. Leonard won world titles in five different weight classifications.

APRIL 6, 1896

King George I of Greece opened the first modern-day Olympic Games in Athens. Around 245 men from 14 countries competed in 9 events. Most of the competitors were Greek. Event winners were given an olive branch, a certificate, and a silver medal. The Americans were by far the most successful team in Athens. The first man to win an Olympic competition was the American James Brendan Connolly, who took the triple jump.

APRIL 23, 1989

The Atlanta Falcons drafted Florida State University's Deion "Prime Time" Sanders as their first-round NFL draft pick. Sanders was given his nickname in high school by

Richard Fain, an athletic rival. Fain went on to play at the University of Florida and in the NFL with a couple of teams as a defensive back.

On September 10, 1989, when he was with the Falcons, Sanders brought a punt back 68 yards for a touchdown against the Rams in his NFL debut. Like Bo Jackson, Sanders was a two-sport pro athlete. Just five days before the touchdown, as a New York Yankee, Sanders homered, hit two doubles, and drove in four runs against Seattle.

Sanders then cut his baseball season short by signing a four-year, $4.5 million contract with Atlanta only three days before the season opener with the L.A. Rams.

While at FSU, Sanders played for the Seminoles in the first game of the Metro Conference tournament in baseball, then went over to the track to run a leg on the 4 × 100-meter relay team while wearing his baseball pants. He next went back to the baseball diamond and had the game-winning hit for FSU in the second game of the day.

DREAM TEAM I
BASEBALL

When you are talkin' sports, a good thing to have in your back pocket is a knowledge of the best of all time. Why? Because it's always a good crutch when somebody says, "That guy is the greatest." And you say, "No, Joe DiMaggio was the greatest," and then explain. Eventually, you will find yourself in a situation where these sports-knowledge-intensive people will sit around and compare this person to that person. The kind of thing sports fans love to do is go back in time and figure out who is the greatest at each position. Pretty impressive? Actually, it is usually pretty boring . . . unless you can come in loaded. Let's start with baseball.

OUTFIELD

BABE RUTH. Easy, right? Nobody had a bigger impact on the game. You never hear anybody say he's the Barry Bonds of basketball or the Albert Belle. No, it's Babe every time. So big, Michael Jordan is referred to as the Babe Ruth of our time: 714 home runs, .342 career hitting average, 54 or more home runs four different seasons. How many athletes can you identify by his nickname?

TED WILLIAMS. People used to show up early to watch him take batting practice at Fenway Park. Last player to finish over .400. Two triple crowns, two MVP awards, six batting crowns. Unbelievable left-hand swing.

JOE DiMAGGIO. The Yankee Clipper. Nobody will match his 56-game hitting streak. Most graceful player ever. Three-time MVP. 361 home runs. Hit .325 career. How can you leave out a guy who was married to Marilyn Monroe?

HANK AARON. Baseball's all-time home run king with 755. Selected to 25 All-Star Games. 2,297 RBIs and 3,771 hits.

TY COBB. The Georgia Peach was a fierce competitor who arrived with his sharpened spikes always flying high. In 24 seasons he hit .367, baseball's highest lifetime average. (Williams finished with .344.) Twelve batting titles, stole 892 bases in his career, and kept trainers in practice taping up spiked ankles.

AROUND THE HORN

FIRST BASE: Lou Gehrig. The Iron Horse. Played in 2,130 straight games. First player in this century to hit four home runs in one game. .340 average. 493 homers. 1,990 RBIs. Teamed up with Babe Ruth to form an awesome one-two punch. In his four-homer game, he just missed a fifth when he flew out to deep center. Still holds record with 23 grand slams. Five times he had 159-plus RBIs in a season.

SECOND BASE: Joe Morgan. Little guy, 5'7" and 150 pounds, but he could play. Drove the Big Red Machine to the 1975 and '76 World Series titles. Back-to-back MVP Awards in '75–'76. One of baseball's most patient hitters. 1,865 walks and 689 stolen bases.

Known for flapping his elbow as he awaited the pitch in the batter's box. This worked as a timing device for him.

SHORTSTOP: Cal Ripken, Jr. Moved to third base in 1997, where he had begun his career in 1981. Baltimore's Cal Ripken, Jr., is truly a charm in the Charm City. In September

1995 the 6'4" Ripken broke what was thought to be an unbreakable feat: Lou Gehrig's consecutive-games-played streak. He was baseball's first really big-in-stature shortstop. Rookie of the Year in 1982, two-time MVP.

THIRD BASE: Mike Schmidt. You'll get all kinds of arguments here. People will be screaming Brooks Robinson, Graig Nettles, Eddie Mathews, but you'll stick with three-time MVP Schmidt, who led the Philadelphia Phillies to their only world championship, in 1980. He finished a brilliant career with 548 home runs, including four in a game, and 1,595 RBIs.

CATCHERS AND PITCHERS

CATCHER: Johnny Bench. Your sports-friendly neighbors will wonder why you don't go with Mickey Cochrane or Yogi Berra, but you are sticking with the guy who set the standards for catchers. Number 5 had a big gun for an arm and 389 home runs. He was MVP twice and Rookie of the Year in 1968. His hands were so big he could hold seven baseballs in one of them. Now there's a conversation stopper—or starter.

RIGHT-HANDED PITCHER: Cy Young. If someone's arguing with you that you're wrong, say "The Babe Ruth of pitchers." Young won 511 games in 815 starts, threw 750 complete games, and won 20 games a season 15 times. Another good argument: The award for the pitcher of the year was named after him.

LEFT-HANDED PITCHER: Warren Spahn. Just say Sandy Koufax retired too early, and end that argument. Spahn won 363 games and had 382 complete games. Twelve times he won 20 or more games a season, and he hurled 63 shutouts. Willie Mays hit his first career home run off Spahn.

RELIEF PITCHER: Dennis Eckersley. Eck. In 1992, as a *relief* pitcher, he was named MVP and Cy Young winner. He compiled 320 saves with the A's. Also known for a mistake: the Kirk Gibson home run that won Game 1 of the World Series for the Dodgers in 1988 was a Dennis Eckersley slider.

MANAGER: Casey Stengel. Who else could you pick to manage this group? Casey managed the Yankees from 1949 to 1960. He also managed Brooklyn, Boston, and the New York Mets in the National League. In 25 years in the dugout, he won 1,905 games. You're also going to want to put Tommy Lasorda in the dugout for the stories.

You're gonna love May because this month you get to drop some of the biggest names in baseball. From Babe Ruth and Lou Gehrig, to Stan Musial and Rickey Henderson, to Nolan Ryan and Bo Belinsky, to Mamie Van Doren and Willie Mays. Let's begin with Willie since it is May.

MAY 28, 1951

After going hitless in his first 12 major-league at-bats, New York Giants outfielder Willie Mays hit his first career homer, off Boston Braves' left-hander Warren Spahn.

It was Mays's first career hit. How about this: The "Say Hey Kid" hit 660 career regular-season homers (the third most in baseball history). In 71 at-bats, spread over four World Series appearances, Mays failed to homer even once. In fact, he had just three extra-base hits, all doubles.

You'll find that Cal Ripken, Jr.'s name is brought up more than ever these days for a couple of reasons. He is baseball's Iron Man—with the longest consecutive-game streak—and he's still running. And he's a great guy. I mean a genuine great guy. So when his name comes up in May, you bring up May 2, 1939, when New York Yankee Lou Gehrig took himself out of the lineup to end his record streak of consecutive games at 2,130. The streak had begun on June 1, 1925. The 35-year-old was suffering from unexplained weakness and sluggishness, which was later diagnosed as amyotrophic lateral sclerosis, now commonly known as "Lou Gehrig's disease." The Iron Horse died in 1941.

By the way, Cal's first major-league stolen base was a steal of home on May 31, 1982, against Texas. In high school in Aberdeen, Maryland, Cal was a two-time letterman in soccer and won All-County and All-Metro honors. Hard to fathom that Cal was just the forty-eighth overall pick in the 1978 major-league draft. (Kind of like Jordan lasting until the third pick for the Bulls.)

His wife, Kelly, was a pretty good hoops player, who finished second in the state of Maryland in a basketball skills competition in 1973 at age 14. The finals were held at halftime of a Baltimore Bullets game.

Cal has watched the movie *The Silence of the Lambs* more than 20 times.

When the subject of streaks comes up, you go to May 31, 1937, when the Brooklyn Dodgers beat the New York Giants' Carl Hubbell, snapping his major-league record 24-game winning streak. Hubbell had not lost since July 13, 1936. He finished 1936 with 16 straight wins and won 8 more in a row in 1937.

MAY 26, 1959

Pittsburgh Pirate Harvey Haddix pitched 12 perfect innings, retiring 36 batters in a row, against the Milwaukee Braves, but lost the game 1–0 in 13 innings. In the thirteenth, Felix Mantilla got on base on a throwing error. Joe Adcock hit an apparent home run but ended up with a double after passing a base runner. The Braves' Lew Burdette got the win, after surrendering 12 hits.

MAY 2, 1917

Cincinnati Reds pitcher Fred Toney and Chicago Cubs pitcher James "Hippo" Vaughn both pitched nine no-hit innings. The Reds scored a run on two hits in the top of the tenth to win 1–0. Toney fanned the final two batters to complete his no-hitter.

MAY 9, 1984

You're up late watching a game. Not because *you* want to but because your sports-fan friends are stuck on the game. It gets later and later and later. Even your friends ask, "Geez, how much longer can this game go on?" You go to May 9, 1984, when the White Sox and the Milwaukee Brewers played to a 7–6 finish. The story here, though, is that the game set a major-league time record of eight hours, six minutes and is the American League's longest-ever game by innings. Play had been suspended after 17 innings at 1:05 A.M. for the American League curfew. Harold Baines hit a home run in the twenty-fifth inning to give Chicago the victory, and Tom Seaver picked up the win.

MAY 1, 1991

Anytime any discussion of any pitcher comes up, go to Nolan Ryan. In May you can go to May Day, 1991, on Arlington Appreciation Night in Texas, when Texas Ranger Ryan threw his major-league record seventh no-hitter. Ryan struck out 16 Toronto Blue Jays while walking only two. At 44 years old, Ryan is the oldest pitcher to throw a no-no.

On the same day, Rickey Henderson of the A's stole third base off Yankee pitcher Tim Leary and catcher Matt Nokes. It was stolen base number 939 for him, which bested Lou Brock's major-league record. Henderson pulled the base out of the ground and held it over his head. Brock came onto the field to congratulate him. Additionally, in 1982, Henderson broke Brock's record for steals in a season with 130.

MAY 5, 1962

Nolan Ryan threw four no-hitters as a pitcher for the California Angels, but Bo Belinsky threw the franchise's first no-no on this date against Baltimore. Then known as the Los Angeles Angels, the team shared Dodger Stadium with the L.A. Dodgers in 1962. Anaheim Stadium didn't open for baseball until 1966. Jim Fregosi had the first-ever hit at their new stadium, doubling in the first inning off Chicago White Sox starter Tommy John. The ChiSox won the game 3–1 on April 19, 1966. Fregosi was traded to the New York Mets in 1971 for Nolan Ryan and three other players. Belinsky was one of four American League pitchers to hurl a no-hitter that season. That was the most no-hitters in one season in the league since 1917, when five were thrown. Belinsky, a southpaw, went just 28–51 in his eight-year career for five different teams. A colorful player, Belinsky led a playboy lifestyle off the field, dating Ann-Margret, Connie Stevens, and Tina Louise. He also had a much-publicized romance with actress Mamie Van Doren. In '62, Belinsky also issued a league-high 122 bases on balls! Detroit Tigers pitcher Virgil "Fire" Trucks threw two no-hitters in 1952, winning both games 1–0. Then you say, "Trucks was just 5–19 that season."

Every now and then you'll see a teammate stick up for another in professional sports. Not often, these days, but it does happen. With today's salaries, however, you'll never witness what happened on May 18, 1912, when the Detroit Tigers protested the suspension of their star, Ty Cobb, by going on strike and refusing to play the Philadelphia Athletics. Cobb had been suspended for attacking a fan who was heckling him. The fan was missing one hand and part of the other as a result of a workplace accident. The Tigers avoided a $1,000 fine by fielding a replacement team. Aloysius Travers, a 20-year-old seminary student, pitched for Detroit in the 24–2 loss. Travers never pitched in the major leagues again.

American League president Ban Johnson threatened lifetime suspensions from baseball for all striking players. On May 20, Cobb asked his teammates to end the strike. The strike ended, and the players were fined $50 for each day on strike or $100 each.

You can never escape from professional football. Either somebody retires during the spring, a team doesn't get to build a new stadium, a superstar gets married in a secret hideaway, John Madden gets another commercial, or this, which happened on May 7, 1987.

A federal jury ruled that the NFL was in violation of antitrust laws when it attempted to prohibit the Oakland Raiders from moving to Los Angeles. The Raiders played in Oakland from 1960 to 1981 and in Los Angeles from 1982 to 1994. The Raiders have returned to Oakland and played there since the 1995 season.

The Los Angeles Lakers have had a storied career, and usually you will see them in May in the NBA play-offs. Just remind everybody that on May 7, 1972, the Lakers won their first NBA championship by beating the New York Knicks. As the Minneapolis Lakers, the team had won five titles, their last in

1954. The Lakers, however, had lost the finals seven straight times since moving from Minneapolis in 1960.

You can't go anywhere without seeing the Nike Swoosh. Most of the time it's either Tiger Woods or Michael Jordan who comes to mind. The rest of the time its Agassi or Sampras. Then its Monica Seles, Michael Johnson, or Ken Griffey, Jr., and the list continues. Few people ever bring up the first athlete to endorse Nike running shoes. He was Steve Prefontaine, and, on May 30, 1975, he was killed on the Eugene, Oregon, road where he often trained. Although he never broke a world record or won an Olympic medal, Prefontaine set 14 U.S. records during his brief career. An all-American distance runner at Oregon, he was the first athlete to win the same event at the NCAA championship four years in a row. He won the 5,000-meter race from 1970 to 1973.

One month you have Michael Jordan, another you have Muhammad Ali, another Mickey Mantle, another Babe Ruth. In May you can drop a story about the greatest athlete who ever lived.

MAY 5, 1973

Secretariat, ridden by Ron Turcotte, won the Kentucky Derby by two lengths over Sham. It was the fastest Derby ever, as Secretariat won with a time of 1:59⅖. After winning the first jewel in the Triple Crown, Secretariat went on to become one of only 11 horses ever to win the Triple Crown, which consists of the Kentucky Derby, the Preakness Stakes, and the Belmont Stakes. (Forty-one other horses have finished one win shy of the Triple Crown.)

MAY 14, 1919

Sir Barton, ridden by Johnny Loftus, won the Preakness Stakes only four days after winning the Kentucky Derby. The colt remained hot and (June 11, 1919) won the Belmont Stakes to become the first horse to win the Triple Crown. The phrase "Triple Crown," however, was not associated with this particular feat until 1930, when sportswriter Charles Hatton of the *Daily Racing Form* used the phrase in writing about Gallant Fox's victories in the three races. Gallant Fox is the only Triple Crown winner (1930) to sire a Triple Crown winner—Omaha (1935).

MAY 4, 1957

Iron Liege, ridden by Bill Hartack, won the Kentucky Derby by a nose when jockey Bill Shoemaker, riding Gallant Man, overtook it in the stretch but misjudged the finish line. Shoemaker stood up in the saddle at the $\frac{1}{16}$ pole, allowing Iron Liege to regain the lead. When Gallant Man got back in stride, it was too late.

MAY 8, 1915

Regret, ridden by Joe Notter, became the first filly to win the Kentucky Derby. Regret led wire to wire to beat second-place Pebbles by two lengths. Only two other fillies have ever won the Derby, Genuine Risk in 1980 and Winning Colors in 1988. A total of 36 fillies have run in the Derby's history.

MAY 4, 1996

Grindstone won by a nose over Cavonnier to give trainer D. Wayne Lukas an incredible record sixth straight victory in a Triple Crown race. The streak ended in the 1996 Preakness.

The Indianapolis 500 has lost a little of its luster to the boys of NASCAR, and you could probably go through life these days without one Indy story. But if you have to have one or two, you want to talk about Unser and A.J.

MAY 24, 1981

Bobby Unser finished first in the Indy 500, but after the race was penalized one lap for passing illegally under the caution flag. Second-place finisher Mario Andretti was awarded first place, but Unser and car owner Roger Penske appealed the decision to the U.S. Auto Club. After four months, the ruling was overturned and Unser was fined $40,000 but, more important, was again declared the winner.

MAY 29, 1977

A. J. Foyt won his fourth Indy 500, becoming the first driver to accomplish the feat. Also in 1977, Janet Guthrie became the first woman to race in the Indy 500, although she only completed 27 laps because of mechanical problems. Rick Mears and Al Unser, Sr., have also each won four Indy 500s. In 1992, Lyn St. James became the second woman to qualify for the Indy 500, in which she finished eleventh.

Mother's Day is in May, so we offer you a couple of reasons why athletes always say "Hi, Mom" instead of "Hi, Dad." For one, Mom probably always took the player to practice, washed the uniform, put up with schedules, drove in the car pool, quit her job to do the above, got another one to afford college, and the list goes on. Dads—certainly not the modern-day ones—only showed up at a game or two. Now if they can't go, they have it videotaped. By Mom. So on Mother's Day, here's the Mother of Mother stories.

MAY 14, 1939

Cleveland pitcher Bob Feller's parents traveled from Van Meter, Iowa, to Chicago to watch him pitch on Mother's Day. With Feller pitching in the third inning, a foul from Marv Owen struck Feller's mother, broke her glasses, and cut her over her right eye, requiring six stitches. After seeing if his mother was okay, Feller returned to strike out Owen.

MAY 25, 1935

Babe Ruth hit the final three home runs of his career (numbers 712, 713, and 714) in a game at Forbes Field in Pittsburgh. Ruth hit two-run homers in the first and third innings and a solo shot in the seventh. His last homer cleared the right-field grandstand—600 feet away from the plate—cleared the roof, and flew out of the ballpark for the longest ball ever hit at Forbes Field. Ruth retired on June 2, 1935.

MAY 2, 1954

St. Louis Cardinal Stan Musial hit five homers and drove in nine runs in a doubleheader against the New York Giants. Musial set the major-league mark with 21 total bases in two consecutive games and tied the major-league record with five homers in two consecutive games.

MAY 9, 1984

Harold Baines hit a home run in the twenty-fifth inning to lead the Chicago White Sox past the Milwaukee Brewers, 7–6. The game set a major-league time record of eight hours, six minutes and is the American League's longest-ever game by innings. Play had been suspended after 17 innings at 1:05 A.M. for the American League curfew. The game was finished the following day as Tom Seaver recorded the win.

MAY 8, 1984

On the day the Olympic torch relay began, the Soviet Union announced that it would boycott the

1984 Summer Olympic Games. The Soviet National Olympic Committee stated that the country would not be competing because of "the gross flouting" of the Olympic ideals by U.S. authorities.

MAY 17, 1992

Betsy King shot 267 to win the LPGA championship by 11 strokes. King shot rounds of 68, 66, 67, and 66 to become the first LPGA player to finish all four rounds under 70 in a major championship.

TALKIN' SPORTS 101

Inevitably, you are going to get yourself involved in a sports conversation. It may happen today. It may happen tomorrow. It *is* going to happen. In this day and age, sports seeps into everything. Presidents use sports metaphors like "The ball is in Iraq's court."

Political candidates, some of whom are actual sports heroes from the past, throw out sports clichés as if somebody is going to throw money back, for instance, "The quarterback runs the show." Your boss might start a meeting with something like "Jesus, Elway gets injured in an exhibition game. How stupid can they get?" Your brother-in-law is over to your house for a visit. Out of nowhere he says: "Chamberlain or Russell?" What are you supposed to do? Aunt Vera runs into you on the street. You have coffee and catch up, and as a kid walks by with the number 19 on his jersey, she says: "Montana had a nice butt." Your date is obsessed with hockey. He even knows who Foster Hewitt is. Because of this, he sprinkles his conversation with the phrase "He shoots, he scores." (Hewitt is the Canadian announcer who came up with this little ditty after a goal.) A coworker might come up with something like this: "Was it North Carolina or North Carolina State that broke up UCLA's streak?" I mean, you're thinking: "Now what?" And you're right. It never ends with these folks. They are insensitive to the less knowledgeable around them. But this doesn't have to happen anymore. Because you are going to learn how to play a little game that requires very little knowledge of sports but a whole lot of B.S.

Now, some practical hints. Don't get involved in something you can't handle. There's nothing worse than talking sports and getting something wrong. The junkies will jump on you, and you will never recover. So what you want to do is take a broad stroke. Go basic. Don't fight them. They'll only get worse. Example:

"Was it North Carolina or North Carolina State that broke up UCLA's streak?" Now, what this person is talking about is college basketball. The National Championship. From 1964 to 1975, UCLA dominated the sport, winning ten NCAA titles. It was an unbelievable streak that will probably never be repeated. But the championships weren't consecutive. After winning two, Texas Western won in 1966. (Bobby Joe Hill was the MVP.) Then UCLA peeled off another seven in a row, but that streak was broken up by NC State in 1974. So the know-it-all who brought this up is dealing with a lot of information you don't have. This happens a lot.

Let's break it down. We all know, of course, that Notre Dame snapped a UCLA 88-game winning streak. One of the Carolinas spoiled a much smaller streak. Here's your conversation:

"Was it North Carolina or North Carolina State that broke up UCLA's streak?" Now, you can go three ways here. You can simply say, "You know, I don't know and I really don't care and I hate California." Or you can try to bully *your* way into the conversation. Or you can B.S. the conversation into something *you* know about.

The "I don't know, I don't care" thing is your decision. But I have the feeling you would not be reading this right now if that's your choice.

Bullying yourself into this is not a good idea. Let's say you decide to guess and say "North Carolina." Well, for one thing, you're wrong, and in this situation you can get trapped. Because now it opens up the opposing party to say something like "Was the Dean with the Tar Heels then?" Now how lost are you? Huh? And let's say you guess the correct answer and say, "NC State." They say: "Right. But remember when North Carolina and NC State won it back-to-back?" Now what? So, you see, it doesn't do you any good to enter this battle without weapons. So here's what you do. You get the conversation back to a comfort zone.

"Was it North Carolina or North Carolina State that broke up UCLA's streak?" Well, you are probably smart enough to realize he's talking college something, right? Big clues here are North Carolina, North Carolina State, and UCLA. "What streak?" you're thinking. You could go with something general like: "College ball is great. Much more exciting than the pros." Or, realizing it's college: "You know what, I always thought those guys should get paid." Or maybe you know something about UCLA, like where it is. And maybe you have a general knowledge that Magic Johnson played in Los Angeles as well. There you go, you're off and running: "You know, L.A. hasn't had that much excitement since the Magic years." The key is to get the guy off the trivia. Talk about a relative in North Carolina. Talk about the great weather in California. Talk about any streak you know of. "Boy, Newt Gingrich has been on a rough streak." Just give yourself enough breathing room to get to the next topic.

Let's try a couple more:

"What's your favorite Olympic sport?" Go with something you know about. Like figure skating. Everybody can talk about figure skating. In the smart conversation you miss the compulsories. An obvious conversation is to dig up Tonya Harding and Nancy Kerrigan and your reaction. You can talk about the beauty of the mountains. Your love of track and field. How Richard Jewell got hosed. Or you can say: "All of them." It's a great distraction. Look under February for some tips.

"Do you think Oscar De La Hoya can save boxing?" The answer from any nonimpaired sports fan would be, "Well, he and Roy Jones, Jr., can try, but in this sport, you never know what can happen." And to some extent you—the no-clue fan—could probably talk about boxing at some length. I mean you've heard of Muhammad Ali at some point; you certainly have heard of Mike Tyson. You can even talk about something you saw in one of the Rocky movies. So boxing is always easy. Your answer here might be something like: "I hope so. Ever since Mike Tyson bit off Evander Holyfield's [it's *HOLY*field] ear, they are not getting my money. So yes, I *hope* Oscar can save boxing." The truth is next time Tyson and Holyfield fight, you'll be there along with everybody else. It's like a car crash. You really don't want to look, but you really do.

"Will anybody break Roger Maris's home run record?" Surely you know that Babe Ruth once held a home run record that seemed unbreakable, 60 "dingers" in one season. The record lasted from 1927 to 1961, when Roger Maris hit 61. Hitters have been chasing it since. So your knowledgeable answer is that with diluted pitching due to expansion, it will be easier to get to 62. Ken Griffey, Jr., Mark McGwire, and Tino Martinez have the best shots now. But once you get in the later forties, the pressure is just too much. Your get-me-out-of-here answer has to be a bit more global. You can talk about how difficult it is to break records. You can talk about how the glare of the media makes it too tough to focus on the record. If you remember that Maris broke Babe Ruth's record, you have carte blanche to talk about the old days all you want: how ticket prices used to be affordable, how the athletes were accessible. By the time you're done, your opponent will either be asleep or onto a discussion of the balanced budget.

Now, June means only one thing: the NBA Finals. We say "now" because they used to end in May. In fact, the most famous May NBA Finals ending was on May 16, 1980, when a rookie by the name of Earvin Johnson—that's Magic Johnson to you—filled in for an injured Kareem Abdul-Jabbar and came up with 42 points, 15 rebounds, and 7 assists. It was Game 6 of the finals, an unbelievable evening of entertainment. Here we had the future of the NBA giving us a glimpse of showtime. And how many people watched this momentous event live on national television? None. The game was on tape delay on CBS. Things have changed a little bit since then.

Nevertheless, June is now NBA time, and as you watch the finals with your friends, you'll want to go over some of the games that still stick with us. Like the one on June 4, 1976, when a game for the ages was played in Boston Garden: a three-overtime affair between Boston and Phoenix. Boston outlasted the Suns, 128–126. Jo Jo White led the winners with 33 points. But it was Phoenix's Gar Heard who hit the "shot heard 'round the world" to force a third overtime. Gar played 61 minutes. Jo Jo lasted 60. An unlikely hero in this contest, who nobody ever talks about, was Glenn McDonald, who came off the bench in the third overtime and scored six points down the stretch for Boston. He played only nine more games in the NBA.

On June 13, 1993, for the second time in two decades, Phoenix went into triple overtime in an NBA Finals game. Phoenix beat Michael Jordan and Chicago 129–121, with Kevin Johnson playing 62 minutes and scoring 25 points. The euphoria didn't last long for Phoenix. Three days later Jordan scored

55 points and the Bulls took a 3–1 series lead. Chicago later won its third straight NBA title in Phoenix. Talk about road warriors. The Bulls won all three championship series games *at* Phoenix. Here's another Jordan story you can rely on:

The Bulls' very first NBA title came on June 12, 1991, when they beat the Lakers. Guess who led all scorers? Michael Jordan, with an average of 31 points per game. He also averaged 11 assists and 3 steals a game. You can say he also sold popcorn and parked cars at the stadium. Kidding, of course, but here's a note about Jordan your friends won't know. He once was a clean-up guy at a restaurant called Whitey's in Wilmington, North Carolina. He hated the job.

Michael owns 6 of the top 11 scoring performances in NBA play-off history, including a record 63 in Boston in 1986. This was the game where yours truly had Mr. Jordan on at the beginning of the broadcast. I asked him, "Michael, can one man beat the Lakers?" And he answered, "I don't know, we're playing the Boston Celtics."

❗

OBNOXIOUS POINT
Michael was selected to eight NBA all-defensive first teams. The only other person to do this was Bobby Jones of the Philadelphia 76ers, who played with epilepsy.

MJ greatest quote ever: After being elected by broadcasters to the all-interview team for the fourth consecutive year, we asked him how he felt about this honor. His answer: "No comment."

Speaking of the Lakers, their biggest rival was the Boston Celtics. Over a span of 25 years, Boston defeated the Lakers eight times in the NBA Finals (once in Minneapolis and seven times in L.A.). In 1985, Boston won Game 1 by 34 points, scoring an NBA Finals record 148 points at the Boston Garden. Three days later L.A. came back and shocked Boston at home. The Lakers finally won the series in seven. (You're always supposed to win your home games. Don't forget to note if a game is home or away. If a team loses at home, groan for at least ten seconds and say something like, "There goes the home-court advantage.") Anyway, again in Boston, up three games to two, Kareem Abdul-Jabbar scored 29 points and the Lakers won the series. The breakthrough had happened. Laker fans will always remember June of 1985.

The very next year Boston and Los Angeles played a series that was historic for a couple of reasons. One, it went a grueling seven games. And two, you can safely say it was the series in which the NBA became really physical. This was the series, in June of 1986, when Boston's Kevin McHale took down L.A.'s Kurt Rambis with a clothesline tackle in Game 4 and the intensity in basketball from that moment went up a notch. By the way, Larry Bird had 21 rebounds in the same game. Two days later, in Game 5, Larry had 34 points in the Boston Garden, where it was 97 degrees.

Fiction or fact? It was always rumored that Boston's legendary coach, Red Auerbach, turned off the air-conditioning in the Laker locker room. But I don't think there was any there in the first place in the old Garden. It's a good story though. It was also believed that Red arranged to have the tunnel from the airport blocked so Kareem, who suffered from terrible headaches, had to breathe in car fumes. This was never confirmed, but the Laker bus got stuck in the tunnel that year. Speaking of fumes, Red lit his usual victory cigar after the seven-game series.

OBNOXIOUS POINT
Boston is 16–3 in the NBA Finals.

JUNE 21, 1988

Los Angeles became the first team since Boston in 1968–69 to repeat as NBA champions, beating Detroit 108–105 in a decisive Game 7, in which "Big Game" James Worthy scored 36 points. In Game 6, despite 36 points from Isiah Thomas, L.A. rallied behind two free throws by Abdul-Jabbar, who was fouled by Bill Laimbeer with 14 seconds left. The only problem was, and I was standing there, Bill was about six feet from Kareem when he "fouled" him. After the game, Magic Johnson was so happy he actually picked me up as I was interviewing him live on television.

L.A. coach Pat Riley made good on his "guarantee" to win back-to-back titles. (See January and Joe Namath and Riley). By the way, the Lakers haven't won an NBA title since. The Celtics have suffered longer—since 1986.

June is the month when major-league baseball hits the 50-game mark, so the season is well under way by then. A third under way, to be nearly exact. The season is 162 games loooooong. So every now and then baseball teams and their marketing departments get bored. You'll hear about free-baseball days—well, not anymore—they've been banned after a game had to be stopped last spring in Milwaukee when overzealous fans (often you can read that as drunk fans) threw their free baseballs at the visiting Texas Rangers. Well, in 1974 the Cleveland Indians held a ten-cent beer-night promotion. With the score tied at five–five in the ninth inning, drunken fans, or overzealous fans, came out on the field and began to disrupt the action. Things got out of control. The game was forfeited to the Texas Rangers, who at one point stormed out of the dugout to take on the drunks. That's baseball.

You can celebrate any baseball conversation with the following.

JUNE 8, 1968

L.A. Dodgers pitcher Don Drysdale stretched his consecutive scoreless innings streak to 58⅔ before Philadelphia's Howie Bedell finally drove in a run with a sacrifice fly. Drysdale posted six consecutive shutouts during the streak. It was Bedell's only RBI of the season. In fact, he had only three in his 67-game major-league career. Meanwhile, Drysdale played only one more year after his record-breaking season. The runner who scored on Bedell's sacrifice fly? Tony Taylor. Who caught Bedell's sacrifice fly? Left fielder Len Gabrielson.

JUNE 10, 1944

Cincinnati's Joe Nuxhall, at age 15, became the youngest player ever to appear in a major-league game as he pitched in the ninth inning against the St. Louis Cardinals. He was then sent to the minors before coming back in 1952. Nuxhall went on the win 135 games in his career and even hit 15 homers in 766 at-bats!

JUNE 15, 1938

Cincinnati southpaw Johnny Vander Meer hurled a 6–0 no-hitter against the Dodgers at Brooklyn's Ebbets Field. It was Vander Meer's second straight hitless pitching performance. He had no-hit Boston four days earlier. (The Boston Braves, not Red Sox). Vander Meer struck out seven and walked eight in his historic no-hitter against the Dodgers. Along with Vander Meer's no-hitter that night, it was also the first-ever night game at Ebbets Field. Plagued by wildness throughout his career, Vander Meer won 119 games and lost 121 over a 13-year career.

JUNE 17, 1962

New York Mets first baseman "Marvelous" Marv Throneberry hit an apparent triple against the Chicago Cubs but was called out for failing to touch first and second base! Officially, he was out for missing first base. When manager Casey Stengel went out to argue, the umpire told him Throneberry had missed second base as well. The Mets went 40–120 in their first season in 1962. Throneberry symbolized their ineptness. Officially Marvin Eugene Throneberry, his initials fittingly spelled MET. His older brother, Faye, an outfielder, played eight seasons in the big leagues. Marv played seven and had an overall batting average of .237. He later became popular on Miller Lite beer commercials on television and once said, "I still don't know why they asked me to do this commercial." He died of cancer at age 60 in June 1994, leaving behind five children, ten grandchildren, and four great-grandchildren.

JUNE 19, 1889

Washington Statesmen outfielder Dummy Hoy threw out three Indianapolis base runners at home plate in one inning. Hoy, who was deaf, played 14 years in the big leagues. He was the reason umpires started using hand signals along with vocal calls of "strike," "safe," and "out."

JUNE 2, 1941

Lou Gehrig, the Iron Horse, died in New York City at the age of 37 from amyotrophic lateral sclerosis, which is now called "Lou Gehrig's disease." Gehrig held the record of 2,130 consecutive games played before Cal Ripken, Jr., broke it in 1995. Gehrig's streak began on June 1, 1925, when he pinch-hit for Pee Wee Wanninger. The next day, Wally Pipp, the Yankees' regular first baseman, sat out a game with a headache. Gehrig replaced him and went on to set the consecutive-games streak. Wally Pipp's name often comes up when a player is hurt and his substitute fills in with success. Despite being overshadowed by Babe Ruth, Gehrig was a great player in his own right. He hit .340 for his career and had 493 career home runs, including 23 grand slams! He won the Triple Crown in 1934, leading the American League in homers, RBIs, and batting average. On July 4, 1939, shortly after being diagnosed with ALS, Gehrig was honored at Yankee Stadium by his team. It was then that he made the famous speech in which he said, "Today, I consider myself the luckiest man on the face of the earth."

A little quiz here. Who's the greatest athlete ever according to this book? Secretariat.

JUNE 9, 1973

Secretariat won the Belmont Stakes by the improbable margin of 31 lengths over Twice A Prince and in the process won horse racing's first Triple Crown in 25 years. Citation, ridden by Eddie Arcaro, wrapped up the Triple Crown on June 12, 1948. Thirty-one-year-old Canadian-bred jockey Ron Turcotte guided Secretariat to the milestone win.

A milestone for female jockeys in June was Julie Krone.

JUNE 5, 1993

Julie Krone, aboard Colonial Affair, won the Belmont Stakes, the final jewel in racing's Triple Crown. The win was the first-ever for a woman in a Triple Crown event. Krone made her Kentucky Derby debut in 1992. In 1970, Diane Crump became the first female jockey to ride in the Kentucky Derby. Krone, aboard Ecstatic Ride, finished fourteenth out of 18 horses in the '92 Derby.

JUNE 10, 1978

Affirmed and jockey Steve Cauthen won the Triple Crown, nipping Alydar at the Belmont Stakes. Cauthen, from Walton, Kentucky, burst onto the scene at age 17 in 1977, and ended his career with 487 wins. It was the closest Belmont finish since 1962 when Jaipur beat Admiral's Voyage by a nose. Affirmed became the third Triple Crown winner in six years. In 1985, Cauthen checked into a drug and alcohol rehab center.

With summer arriving this month, you'll be buying a new bicycle. While you're shopping at your local bike shop, drop these two stories.

JUNE 17, 1945

Bicycling great Eddy Merckx was born in Belgium in the village of Meensel-Kiezegem. Merckx got started at the age of four on a little bike with fat tires and won his first race on October 1, 1961, at Lettelingen in the debutants category. He appeared in his first Tour de France in 1969 and won it.

Merckx says he rode, on an average, 35,000 kilometers a year and that he probably rode a total of 500,000 kilometers over his career! (That means he rode the equivalent of 12 times around the world!) He won the Tour de France five times, including four wins in a row from 1969 to 1972. He returned in '74 and won it. He finished his career in 1978.

JUNE 26, 1961

Greg LeMond was born. Skiing was originally LeMond's sport. In 1985, he finished in second place in the Tour de France. In 1986, he became the first American to win the race. He came back from injuries to win it again in 1989 and 1990. *Sports Illustrated* named him its Sportsman of the Year in 1989.

June is also the month O. J. Simpson was arrested for the murders of his wife and her friend. O.J. also played football. See December. At about the same time . . .

JUNE 14, 1994

The New York Rangers ended a 54-year Stanley Cup drought when they defeated Vancouver 3–2 to win the best of seven series four games to three and capture the cup. Rangers defenseman Brian Leetch became the first U.S.-born player to win the Conn Smythe Trophy as play-off MVP. Before their 1994 win, New York had last won the Stanley Cup in 1940 when it defeated Toronto four games to two. Three of the Rangers' four game-winning goals in the 1940 series win came in overtime!

The Stanley Cup, the oldest trophy professional athletes in North America compete for, was donated by Frederick Arthur Stanley, Lord Stanley of Preston and son of the Earl of Derby, in 1893. Lord Stanley purchased the trophy for ten guineas ($50 at that time) for presentation to the amateur hockey champions of Canada.

JUNE 10, 1977

Golfer Al Geiberger set a PGA Tournament record when he shot a round of 59 at the Danny Thomas Memphis Classic. Geiberger's round included 11 birdies, 1 eagle, and a total of 23 putts. He won the tournament by three strokes, posting rounds of 72, 59, 72, and 70. The score of 59 was equaled in 1991 by Chip Beck at the Las Vegas Invitational.

July

July is a great month in sports because you don't have a lot to focus on. Oh, you can take some June basketball stories and carry them over, but for the most part, you want to bone up on some baseball tomes, and, after you throw in a couple of Wimbledon stories, you're set. By the way, say this word a couple of times before you use it in public. It's Wimbledon. Wimble*done*. You'll hear announcer after announcer refer to it as Wimbleton, as I once did before a Brooks Brothers–clad fan approached me, grabbed my jaw, and said it's *done! done! Wimbledone!*

So anyway, here we are in July and baseball is in the air and so is the smell of gunpowder. It's the month baseball parks step up their fireworks budgets.

As for you, you'll be at office picnics, you'll be at the beach, you'll be sitting at some outdoor patio eatery—and you'll be telling the following stories.

"There are some records that will never be beaten." You can say that, even though we know it's not true. As long as there's a human race and gymnasiums, somebody, somewhere, is training to break records. All he or she needs along the way is to be healthy and incredibly talented—and have a little luck. But somebody's going to need a lot of luck to beat a record that was set in July of 1947.

JULY 17, 1947

New York Yankee Joe DiMaggio's major-league-record 56-game hitting streak ended, against the Cleveland Indians. During the streak, which began on May 15, the Yankee Clipper batted .408, and had 91 hits, including 15 homers and 55 RBIs. He ended up five games shy of his own 1933 Pacific Coast League consecutive-games hitting streak. In his next game, July 18, he started a second streak that lasted 16 games for a combined streak of 72 out of 73 games with a hit.

JULY 20, 1976

Hank Aaron hit home run number 755, the last homer of his career. According to *I Had a Hammer,* Aaron's autobiography, Dick Arndt of the Milwaukee Brewers ground crew grabbed it and got fired when he refused to return it. Aaron stated that he calls Arndt "every few years" to try and buy the ball from him, offering up to $10,000.

JULY 18, 1987

New York Yankee Don Mattingly homered in his eighth straight game to tie Dale Long's 1956 major-league record, which was tied again on July 28, 1995, by Ken Griffey, Jr. At Arlington Stadium in Texas, the crowd of 41,871 called Mattingly out of the dugout for an ovation. Mattingly had ten home runs during the eight-game stretch.

JULY 7, 1937

New York Yankee pitcher Vernon "Lefty" Gomez got his major-league-record third All-Star Game victory as the American League beat the National League 8–3 in Washington's Griffith Stadium. Teammate Lou Gehrig provided the offense with a homer and four RBIs. Losing pitcher Dizzy Dean broke his right big toe on Earl Averill's line drive. Franklin Delano Roosevelt becomes the first president to attend an All-Star Game and throw out the first pitch.

JULY 9, 1969

Chicago Cub Jimmy Qualls blooped a single off Mets pitcher Tom Seaver with one out in the top of the ninth inning to spoil Seaver's perfect game. Seaver went on to win the game 4–0 before a then record crowd of 59,083 at Shea Stadium. No Mets pitcher had ever thrown a no-hitter. As a member of the Reds, Seaver finally threw a no-hitter against St. Louis on June 16, 1978. Qualls played three seasons in the big leagues for 3 different clubs. He hit .223 in 63 career games with zero home runs.

JULY 24, 1983

Toward the end of the month, baseball had one of its most controversial games ever. The New York Yankees and the Kansas City Royals were in the ninth inning with the Yanks up 4–3. George Brett of the Royals hit a two-run homer off Goose Gossage and KC took the lead. Yankee manager Billy Martin protested the amount of pine tar on Brett's bat, and home-plate umpire Tim McClelland called Brett out because the pine tar was more than 18 inches from the base of the bat. Brett exploded, charged onto the field, and had to be restrained. Royals manager Dick Howser protested the game, and American League president Lee MacPhail agreed, overruling the umpire and awarding Brett the two-run homer. On August 18, the game was finished from the point of the protest and the Royals emerged triumphant 5–4.

JULY 24, 1993

New York Mets pitcher Anthony Young walked home the winning run with two outs in the tenth inning to give the L.A. Dodgers a 5–4 win. Young's twenty-seventh straight loss set a major-league-record (his losing streak lasted from May 6, 1992, to July 24, 1993). After the game, Mets outfielder Vince Coleman threw a firecracker from a parked car at fans seeking autographs, injuring a woman and two children.

JULY 28, 1993

Mets pitcher Anthony Young won in relief against the Florida Marlins, breaking his major-league-record 27-game losing streak. Boston Braves pitcher Cliff Curtis had previously held the record, losing 23 in a row in 1910 and 1911. During Young's streak, he was 0–14 as a starter and 0–13 as a reliever. Despite losing those 27 games, he did rack up 15 saves along the way! (Saves don't end a losing streak—only a win can.) Young came on in relief of starter Bret Saberhagen in the ninth inning with the score tied at 2–2. Florida scored an unearned run off Young in the top of the ninth, but the Mets plated two runs off ace reliever Bryan Harvey in their half to win it. Young lost his last 14 decisions in 1992 and his first 13 in 1993. How about Minnesota's Terry Felton? He lost his first 16 career decisions in the big leagues. His winless span went from April 18, 1980, to September 12, 1982, and his record was 0–16 in 55 appearances, with a 5.53 ERA.

Cy Young holds the career record for losses with 315 in his 22-year career. He also won 511 career games, a major-league record.

You can always fire up a conversation by bringing up the name George Steinbrenner, the Yankee owner. I actually like George and can get into more arguments about him than somebody who walks into a Brentwood, California, bar and says, "Hey, I kinda believe O.J."

JULY 6, 1983

In the fiftieth-anniversary All-Star Game, which was played at Chicago's Comiskey Park (also the site of the first All-Star Game), the American League ended the National League's 11-game winning streak with a 13–3 victory. White Sox president Jerry Reinsdorf was fined $500 for a riddle he asked at this game: "How do you know when George Steinbrenner is lying?" His answer: "When his lips are moving."

Baywatch stat: On July 17, 1978, Texas pitcher George Medich went into the stands and saved the life of a 61-year-old fan who was suffering a heart attack. Medich, a medical student, administered cardiac first aid until the paramedics arrived. You may know George another way: Doc.

So you're watching your hometown fireworks display. Because it's summer and it doesn't get really dark until around ten, you're cranky, the kids are cranky, the beer's warm, and you're thinking to yourself, Let's get on with it. While you're standing around waiting for the chamber of commerce president to complete his speech, you can remind anybody who is listening about July 4, 1984, when the Mets and the Braves played 19 innings at Atlanta–Fulton County Stadium. The Mets won 14–13. The story here, though, is that the fireworks show went on as planned—after the game. Problem: It was 4 A.M. Local residents called the police and complained.

Hey, speaking of things going wrong . . .

JULY 12, 1979

A Disco Demolition Night at Chicago's Comiskey Park backfired. Fans who brought in disco records received 98-cent tickets to a doubleheader against the Tigers. Fifty thousand fans showed up with records, which were to be burned in a bonfire between games. After the first game, at least 5,000 fans refused to leave the field. After a 1-hour, 16-minute delay and pleas from owner Bill Veeck, the second game was ruled a Tiger victory by forfeit.

WIMBLEDON

Perhaps the greatest memories surround John McEnroe. Not so much because of his great victories there but for his rants and raves and tantrums and long hair tucked under that headband. When John broke through in 1981 in a legendary match with Björn Borg, he took over the sport. One of my favorite moments occurred when Bud Collins, the great tennis announcer and writer, seeing that Mac was wearing a red headband, said: "Stick a feather in his cap and call him McEnroney."

McEnroe was fined for his outbursts at Wimbledon. He also got a telegram from Phil Knight, who was trying to build up his shoe company. (McEnroe was a Nike athlete.) "Keep doing that," Phil wrote. He kept doing it.

JULY 13, 1881

In the fastest final in Wimbledon history, William Renshaw won the first of his six straight Wimbledon singles titles by beating John Hartley 6–0, 6–1, 6–1 in only 37 minutes.

JULY 8, 1967

Billie Jean King won three titles at Wimbledon. She beat Ann Haydon Jones in the singles title, played with Rosie Casals for the women's doubles title, and was victorious with Owen Davidson in the mixed doubles title.

JULY 7, 1985

Boris Becker of West Germany won the men's singles title at age 17 to become the youngest Wimbledon men's singles champion. He also became the first unseeded player ever to win the Wimbledon men's singles title. "Boom Boom" beat Kevin Curran for the title and followed this win up the next year with another singles title, beating Ivan Lendl.

JULY 6, 1957

Althea Gibson of the U.S. became the first African-American to win a championship at Wimbledon when she beat American Darlene Hard to win the women's singles title. Gibson won the Wimbledon singles title again the following year.

In July, if you run across a million dollars, you can cite Citation, who won the final race of his career on the fourteenth and became the first horse to earn a million dollars in career money. It was 1951. Citation won the Triple Crown in 1948—and finished out of the money just once in 45 starts, earning a total of $1,085,760. Use Citation when you are saying something is a good bet.

On July 13, 1996, Cigar tied Citation's modern-day record of 16 consecutive victories with his win at the Arlington Citation Challenge. Cigar's streak was broken in his next race, the Pacific Classic, where he placed third.

Ever win the lottery? Shaquille O'Neal did on July 18, 1996, when he signed with the Los Angeles Lakers for $121 million for seven years. What's he worth in today's market? On July 5, 1968, the Philadelphia 76ers traded Wilt Chamberlain to the Los Angeles Lakers for three players and an undisclosed cash payment. Darrall Imhoff and Archie Clark become members of the 76ers.

FACTOID ON WILT
For years Wilt never wore shoes. That's right—the only shoes he ever wore were tennis shoes. On the street he went barefoot or wore simple sandals. He liked the freedom, and shoes bothered his feet.

July is the month of the Summer Olympics every four years. So usually there's a plethora of track and field stories leading up to July. For example, on July 27, 1993, Cuba's Javier Sotomayor became the first person ever to break the eight-foot mark in the high jump. He reached eight and a half feet, which set the world record.

JULY 31, 1994

Sergei Bubka of the Ukraine raised the world record in the pole vault in Sestriere, Italy. The vault marked the thirty-fifth time in his career that he had raised the world record. The vault of 20 feet, 1¾ inches broke his old mark of 20 feet 1¼ inches.

JULY 24, 1908

On a day you get confused or somebody is going the wrong way, literally or figuratively, remind him of the time Dorando Pietri of Italy led the 1908 Olympic Marathon as he entered the stadium for the final stage of the race. But he was running the wrong way. Officials attempted to redirect him, but he fell four times. Disoriented, he was disqualified when the officials helped him to his feet. John Hayes of the United States then won the race.

There may be no greater Olympic athlete in terms of feats on the field and in terms of making a career out of a good couple of days than Bruce Jenner.

JULY 30, 1976

Bruce Jenner, 26, from San Jose, California, broke the world record en route to winning the gold medal in the decathlon in the 1976 Summer Olympics in Montreal. Jenner compiled 8,618 points in winning the ten-event, two-day competition. His point total beat the world total of 8,454 points set by Nikolai Avilov of the Soviet Union when he won the 1972 Olympic gold medal at Munich. Jenner had finished tenth at Munich. In winning the gold medal, Jenner set or tied seven personal bests in the ten events.

WHEN SOMEBODY SAYS...
"Boy, I bet he'll hear about that one," referring to a missed shot, a bad pass, a fumble, or another mistake, tell the story of 27-year-old defender Andrés Escobar of Colombia's 1994 World Cup soccer team, who kicked the ball into his own team's net in an opening round 2–1 upset loss to the United States. Ten days later, on July 2, 1994, he was shot 12 times in Medellín, Colombia. Witnesses said the shooter shouted, "Goal, goal," as he fired each shot. Nice.

JULY 17, 1966

Jim Ryun, a sophomore at the University of Kansas, ran a mile in 3:51.3, a staggering 2.3 seconds faster than the previous world record held by France's Michel Jazy. *Sports Illustrated* named Ryun its Sportsman of the Year in 1966. Runner Roger Bannister, a 25-year-old med student, was *SI*'s first-ever Sportsman of the Year, in 1954. On May 6, 1954, Bannister became the first man to run a sub-four-minute mile. At the Iffley Road track in Oxford, England, he ran a 3:59.4 mile.

A WINNER NEVER QUITS, A QUITTER NEVER WINS

Welcome to the pages that will either make you or break you in a crucial situation. No, we're not going to give you the kind of trivia that will make your date propose on sight or pick up the check or follow you home. It is here where you will learn some of the great clichés in sports. Clichés and sports go together like Diego Maradona and controversy. Now see, already you've learned something—a made-up cliché you can use when tying somebody in with something illegal. Maradona was South American soccer Player of the Year twice. He played for Argentina, and, while he was an unbelievable talent on the field, he did like to party and do drugs and all that, and he usually got caught. Let's just say that clichés and sports go together like Maradona and drug testing.

At any rate, what follows are things that, sadly, sportscasters and athletes still use. Really. Let's break them down for you.

"When the going gets tough, the tough get going." Made famous by that football coach wannabe Richard Nixon. But let's think about this for a moment. Is the going really tough in sports when you are playing a kids' game for $20 million? I don't think so.

"He gives 110 percent." Get real here. Where I went to school we only could give 100 percent.

"It ain't over till it's over." When Yogi Berra said this, it was probably cute. Then somebody wrote it down and passed it along and now we hear people in the bottom of the ninth saying this one. First of all, never say "ain't" in public. Second, of course it's not over till it's over. They're going to end the game early? It ain't going to happen.

"What a brick!" This phrase is usually used when a basketball player throws up a shot and hits the rim in such a way that, well, somebody once thought it looked or sounded like a brick. I don't know about you, but I've never heard the sound of a real brick hitting a rim, and I'm here to tell you nobody has tried.

"The whole nine yards." As in "He did it all, the whole nine yards." What makes this disturbing is that you need ten for a first down, so who decided to come up a yard short? Somebody who didn't have the whole nine yards, that's who.

"He came to play." Let me ask you this: Did he come to sell peanuts?

"Take it one day at a time." Usually said after a game, during a slump, by a baseball player who at one time or another was in a 12-step program.

"Winning isn't everything, it's the only thing." Attributed to Vince Lombardi, though it was a college football coach who said it. Still, it's one of those clichés you wouldn't want to use around, say, basketball's Ralph Sampson.

"Win one for the Gipper." Notre Dame fans are about the only ones who might drag this dinosaur out. If I were you, I wouldn't.

"Couldn't hit the broad side of a barn." And he's not trying to, either. He's trying to hit somebody's sinker.

"Nothing but net." Use it only when somebody asks you what you did last night and you were surfing the Internet.

"He gave his all." Meaning he lost.

"**He's athletic.**" Meaning he's white.

"**See the ball, be the ball.**" Meaning he's on acid.

"**Stay within yourself.**" Come on out, the game's not over.

"**Sweating bullets.**" Drank his minibar.

"**It's do or die.**" This one always bothered me. Maybe it's true if you're on Saddam Hussein's softball team, but not for many other sports.

"**You can kiss this one good-bye.**" Why would you say good-bye to a baseball?

"**There's no I in team.**" No, but there's an M and an E.

"**It's not whether you win or lose but how you play the game.**" Well, bud, if you don't play the game well, you lose, so there.

"**He's got his game face on.**" How the hell do we know? He could be thinking about his wife's affair or even how he's going to afford five cars and three Jeeps.

"**Put a fork in it.**" If you say this, eat it, too.

"**Like there's no tomorrow.**" Well, if there's no tomorrow, I'm leaving the stadium to hug my kid.

"**The hot hand.**" Is there a cold hand?

"**Till the cows come home.**" Cows only go where there's food or flies. Stay away from this one.

"**It's not over till the fat lady sings.**" A lame opera connection, but when was the last time you saw a fat lady singing in the stands at Lambeau Field? And the game still ended, right?

"**He's focused.**" He wasn't last time.

"**Just happy to be here.**" No kidding, fella. Because if you weren't here, you'd be a sophomore in college cheating on your exams.

"**Their backs are against the wall.**" Let's think this one out pretty hard, okay. If you were losing in a game, would you actually go stand against a wall? If you are down three games to one in a seven-game series, is your spouse saying, "Honey? Are you going to stand against that wall all day?"

"Slow as molasses in January." Who the heck uses molasses anymore? Who the heck uses this cliché?

"He's in the zone." Used for somebody who's got "the hot hand."

"In the freezer." Now you're getting it. One for "the cold hand."

"He's the real deal." And if he strikes out tomorrow?

"It's not the heat; it's the humidity." As Johnny Carson used to say, "it's hot in my oven, too, but I don't hang out in there."

"Raining cats and dogs." Usually spoken by somebody over 70 who's announcing a baseball rain delay.

"Stop on a dime." Who carries dimes around, anyway?

"Time will tell." Well, yes, it will. But I bet if you're saying this, time's up!

"Cut the mustard." Well, I don't know. I've never tried it. If he's cutting the mustard, he's dumb.

"Take that to the bank." Right! And stand in line for an hour. You may need to update this one to "Take that to the ATM." (But not at night or in an area not inhabited by a lot of people.)

"An eye for an eye and a tooth for a tooth." When watching a Tyson fight.

"Don't push your luck." We're pushing ours, so let's move on.

August is superstar month. This is the month in which you drop some of the biggest names in sports as summer winds down and everybody goes back to school. By the end of this chapter, you'll be up on Tom Seaver, Magic Johnson, Michael Johnson, Bob Cousy, Cal Ripken, Jr., Jesse Owens, Ted Williams, Mary Lou Retton, and the magazine that made them all larger than life, *Sports Illustrated.*

The very first *Sports Illustrated* to hit the stands had a cover date of August 16, 1954. On the cover 23-year-old left-handed third baseman Eddie Mathews of the Milwaukee Braves was shown swinging at a pitch at Milwaukee's County Stadium. The catcher was Wes Westrum. The umpire was Augie Donatelli. The cost of the first issue was all of 25 cents. Seven of *SI*'s 20 covers in 1954 featured animals, including a lion, a bull, a horse, an English setter, and a spoonbill duck.

You are looking at someone who has a lovely necklace. Inexplicably, you say, "Did you know Michael Johnson's Nikes weigh less than that piece of jewelry? In fact, the gold track shoes of the superstar speedster weigh only three ounces." Then go on and spin your story.

AUGUST 1, 1996

Michael Johnson broke the world record in the 200-meter dash with a time of 19.32 at the Summer Olympic

Games in Atlanta. Johnson also won the 400-meter dash, thus becoming the first man in Olympic history to win both the 200 and 400 in the same Games. Johnson set an Olympic record in his 400 victory with a time of 43.49 and broke the world record in the 200 by a staggering .34 of a second. Namibia's Frankie Fredericks ran a blistering 19.68, the third fastest time in history, and still finished second, four meters behind Johnson. It was the largest winning margin in an Olympic 200 since Jesse Owens beat Mack Robinson 20.7 to 21.1 in 1936.

And just to stick with another generation of sprinters, how about Jesse Owens in August of 1936? With Adolf Hitler in the stands, 22-year-old Jesse captured four track and field gold medals at the Berlin Olympics.

AUGUST 9, 1936

In the Berlin Games in 1936, Jesse Owens won the 100-meter dash, long jump, and 200-meter dash, and on this day was the leadoff man in the 4 × 100 relay. Owens wasn't supposed to be a member of the relay team. He was ordered to run when the two Jewish teammates, Marty Glickman and Sam Stoller, were taken off the team. Because of World War II, these were the last Olympics until 1948.

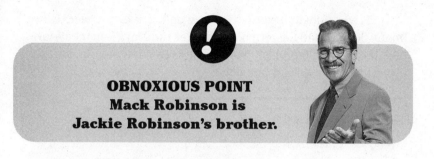

OBNOXIOUS POINT
Mack Robinson is
Jackie Robinson's brother.

AUGUST 5, 1984

The American Joan Benoit pulled away from the pack after just three miles and won the first Olympic women's marathon. Her time of 2:24:52 would have given her victory in 13 of the 20 men's Olympic marathons.

We talked about Bruce Jenner last month as being a premier Olympic athlete, but in no way does this take away from the other premier Olympic athlete, Mary Lou Retton. It was August 3, 1984, at the L.A. Olympics when Mary Lou nailed a perfect ten in the vault to edge out Romania's Ecaterina Szabó and win the gold in the gymnastics women's All-Around championship. Mary needed a perfect vault. There was no getting a 9.9. She later told me she was not nervous because she had performed that move thousands of times, in competition and in practice. No big deal. So when somebody talks about consistency, there you have it. Mary Lou's perfect ten.

The upside, according to Mary Lou, was that she got to meet kings and queens and presidents and was given a new car. The downside was that she got real sick of the song "Hello, Mary Lou."

Trivia question your friends won't ask or answer: How many Soviets and Eastern bloc athletes did Mary Lou meet during the 1984 Olympics? None. They boycotted L.A., so the Americans won 83 gold medals.

AUGUST 6, 1948

Seventeen-year-old Bob Mathias won the decathlon at the Summer Olympics in London. Four years later in Helsinki, he repeated as decathlon Olympic champion. He was the first to win two. Great Britain's Daley Thompson won in 1980 and '84.

Two of the biggest milestones in baseball are 300 career wins as a pitcher and 3,000 hits as a player. Only 21 people have 3,000 hits, and 20 have 300 victories. (By way of comparison, only two have 4,000 hits, Ty Cobb and Pete Rose.) How about two superstars who reached the milestone on the same day? It was August 4, 1985, when Chicago White Sox pitcher Tom Seaver beat the Yankees to win his three-hundredth game. On the same day, California's Rod Carew collected hit number 3,000 against his old team, Minnesota. While Carew got his milestone against the team that originally signed him, Seaver won his game in Yankee Stadium in the Bronx. He had made a name for himself as a member of the New York Mets, pitching 11-plus seasons in Queens. As a member of the Mets, Seaver fanned ten consecutive San Diego batters in 1970.

AUGUST 4, 1982

Speaking of same-day oddities, on this date Joel Youngblood collected base hits for two different teams on the same day: as a New York Mets outfielder, Youngblood got a hit in an afternoon affair with the Cubs. After the game, he was traded to the Montreal Expos in exchange for southpaw Tom Gorman. Youngblood got to Philadelphia hours later and collected a base hit off future Hall of Fame pitcher Steve Carlton. Youngblood played for five National League teams during his 14-year career. Youngblood's hit in the day game versus the Cubs came against Ferguson Jenkins, another future Hall of Famer. Two hits, two different teams, two cities, hits off two future Hall of Famers in one day.

Somebody quotes the Chick Hearn story from the March chapter. Somebody tells you he hasn't missed a bowling night in 50 weeks. Someone tells you she's been to church every Sunday for over a year. And so on. You say that on August 1, 1994, against the Minnesota Twins, Baltimore Orioles shortstop Cal Ripken, Jr., played in his two thousandth consecutive game. The Orioles won the game, 1–0, their first shutout of the season. After going 102 games without a shutout, Baltimore pitchers hurled four in a span of six games! Unfortunately, a work stoppage cut Baltimore and major-league baseball's season short less than a week later.

Magic Johnson was born in August. There are so many emotions attached to Earvin Johnson that it's hard to know where to begin. We can begin here with the fact that he is the man who, for some people, put a face on AIDS for the first time. He turned not being a role model into being a role model after announcing that he was HIV positive. There is nobody, except perhaps Michael Jordan, who has Magic's confidence. He once tried to make a full-court shot at the end of an All-Star Game and when the ball *almost* went in, I said to him, "You didn't expect that to actually go in, did you?" He said, "Irish, I expect them *all* to go in."

AUGUST 14, 1959

Earvin "Magic" Johnson, Jr., was born in Lansing, Michigan, and got his nickname from a Lansing sportswriter, Fred Stabley, Jr., following a 36-point, 18-rebound, 16-assist game for Everett High School. Johnson led Everett to a state title in 1977, played on a high school state champion and an NCAA national championship team, won an NBA ring as a pro, and owns an Olympic gold medal! Johnson was the first overall pick in the 1979 draft after leading Michigan State to the national championship in the spring of 1979, as the Spartans beat Larry Bird and the Indiana State Sycamores. The Lakers acquired the pick to get Johnson as compensation from New Orleans when the Jazz signed free agent guard Gail Goodrich prior to the 1976–77 season. During Johnson's 12-plus season career with the Lakers, he led them to five NBA titles and nine appearances in the NBA Finals. He was an NBA MVP three times and an NBA Finals MVP three times. He played in 11 NBA

All-Star Games and was named MVP twice. As a rookie, on May 16, 1980, Johnson scored 42 points, grabbed 15 rebounds, and handed out 7 assists against Philadelphia in the title-clinching game of the NBA Finals. The Lakers were without injured center Kareem Abdul-Jabbar that night, so Johnson played every position. He was named MVP of those finals, the first and only rookie ever to capture NBA Finals MVP honors. The year before, as a sophomore, Johnson captured the Final Four Most Outstanding Player Award.

If you want to start an argument—and many of you will—read this and make a case that Bob Cousy was better. He wasn't, but you're starting an argument, not ending one.

AUGUST 9, 1928

Bob Cousy was born in New York. Nicknamed the "Houdini of the Hardwood," Cousy revolutionized the point guard position. As a junior at Holy Cross, he won a game against Loyola of Chicago when, with ten seconds left, he got the ball, drove the length of the court, eluded a defender by putting the ball behind his back, and scored a layup. Such fancy dribbling was unheard of at the time. This fancy move was just the start for Cousy. He also made the behind-the-back pass very popular. Cousy, along with Bill Russell, played on six NBA title teams with the Boston Celtics, who won five in a row from 1959 to 1963. He left the Celtics after the '63 season to become basketball coach at Boston College, where he remained for six seasons, winning 117 games and losing just 38 for a .755 percentage. In 1969, he became player-coach of the Cincinnati Royals but played in only seven games, in the 1969–70 season. Along with his NBA titles in Boston, Cousy also played on Holy Cross's 1947 national championship team as a freshman. After his NBA coaching days ended in 1974, Cousy served as commissioner of the American Soccer League from 1975 to 1980. He was the first player from the NBA to grace the cover of *Sports Illustrated,* on January 9, 1956. Cousy was paid $9,000 to play with the 1950–51 Celtics.

With all the talk of Ken Griffey, Jr., breaking Roger Maris's single-season home run record of 61, you can talk about Joe Bauman.

AUGUST 31, 1954

At Roswell, New Mexico, Joe Bauman, playing for Roswell in the Longhorn League, hit four homers against Sweetwater, giving him 68 on the season. He hit four more in his team's remaining six games and finished the minor-league season with 72, a record for an organized baseball season. Joe Hauser of Minneapolis in the Mareican Association in 1933 and Bob Crues of Amarillo in the West Texas–New Mexico League in 1948 had hit 69 homers. In the major leagues, Pittsburgh's Rabbit Maranville holds the record for most at-bats in a season with no home runs. In 1922, he batted 672 times without a homer. He entered that season with 22 career homers.

OBNOXIOUS POINT

Bauman never made it to the major leagues. When he hit his 72 "dingers" in 1954, he also owned a filling station. That's what they used to call gas stations. When his team was in Roswell for a homestand, Bauman would pump gas during the day and hit home runs at night. Despite his record-breaking feat, he didn't receive a raise after the season. We don't know if he did at the gas station.

AUGUST 27, 1982

Oakland's Rickey Henderson stole base 119 of the season versus Milwaukee, breaking Lou Brock's single-season record of 118. The Brewers' pitcher was Doc Medich. The catcher was Ted Simmons, a former teammate of Brock's with St. Louis.

BEST OF THE BEST

In any sports discussion, you'll always be challenged to name the best ever. We're not saying we're right here, but we're close. And when you think about it, it doesn't really matter. Being able to talk sports takes B.S. And that's what we're here for. So somebody says, "He was the greatest of all time," and you begin spreading *your* knowledge.

Here are my picks...

BASKETBALL:
Michael Jordan

BASEBALL:
Babe Ruth

FOOTBALL:
Joe Montana

SOCCER:
Pele

HOCKEY:
Wayne Gretzky

TENNIS:
Rod Laver
Martina Navratilova

TRACK AND FIELD:
Carl Lewis

BOXING:
Muhammad Ali

BOWLING:
Earl Anthony

OLYMPIC ATHLETE:
Mark Spitz

GOLF:
Jack Nicklaus

DIVING:

Greg Louganis

FIGURE SKATING:

Scott Hamilton
Dorothy Hamill

SPEED SKATING:

Eric Heiden

CYCLING:

Eddy Merckx

COLLEGE BASKETBALL COACH:

John Wooden

NBA COACH:

Red Auerbach

COLLEGE FOOTBALL COACH:

Knute Rockne

PRO FOOTBALL COACH:

Vince Lombardi

HOCKEY COACH:

Scotty Bowman

BASEBALL MANAGER:

Casey Stengel

September

In many ways, September is another one of those renewal months in sports. The baseball season is coming to an end, so there is near resolution of that sport. Because we are entering the play-offs and the World Series, everybody is watching the scoreboard to see who is winning, who will go to the postseason. Individual records are being broken and improved on. In some years, the World Series actually got under way. That was when, you say, they didn't drag sports out. The good old days, really. It's one of those months when stars are made because in baseball, anyway, people are stepping up.

For example, September 29, 1954, World Series Game 1: New York Giants versus Cleveland Indians. At the Polo Grounds, New York's Willie Mays amazed the fans when he made the greatest catch in World Series history, a spectacular running grab of Vic Wertz's 440-foot hit with his back to the plate. With two men on, the catch kept the score tied at two–two, and the Giants went on to win 5–2 in the tenth inning on James "Dusty" Rhodes's three-run pinch-hit home run. New York went on to sweep Cleveland in four straight.

September is the month of personal bests. So when somebody is bragging about his favorite player's season, go ahead and take charge.

SEPTEMBER 6, 1995

⚾ Cal Ripken, Jr., broke Lou Gehrig's consecutive-games streak as he played in straight contest number 2,131 for Baltimore. After four and a half innings it was official. Ripken's teammates Rafael Palmeiro and Bobby Bonilla urged him to take a lap around the field. He complied, complete with hugs from players and kisses from his family. After a 22-minute break, the game resumed and Ripken hit a homer in the sixth inning. To put Cal's record in perspective, entering the 1997 season, he had gone 14 straight seasons playing every game. He also played 8,243 straight innings between 1982 and 1987, not including his 82 postseason innings in 1983, when the O's won the World Series. His innings streak was snapped on September 14, 1987, in Toronto when his father, Cal Ripken, Sr., the team's manager, inserted Ron Washington at shortstop in place of Cal, Jr., in the bottom of the eighth inning. The O's lost the game 18–3, giving up a major-league record ten home runs in the loss!

Cal told me, "When I came up in 1981, I sat in the dugout for the first time and watched. I said to myself, "If I ever get a chance to play, I'm never coming out." He hasn't yet . . . for a whole game.

Ripken beat Gehrig's record on September 27, 1923, the same month and day New York Yankee Lou Gehrig hit the first home run of his career, against Bill Piercy of the Boston Red Sox. On the same date 15 years later, Gehrig hit number 493, his final homer, off Dutch Leonard of the Washington Senators.

When you are around real baseball fans, they get legitimately teary-eyed over any discussion of Roberto Clemente because Clemente is the story of unfinished greatness. He has a September history. A final one.

SEPTEMBER 30, 1972

Pittsburgh Pirate Roberto Clemente doubled to left center field off the Mets' Jon Matlack for his three thousandth and final hit. Bill Mazeroski pinch-hit for Clemente in what would have been his last at-bat ever. Clemente was killed in a plane crash on December 31 on his way to deliver relief supplies to victims of the Nicaraguan earthquake. Clemente won the National League batting title four times ('61, '64, '65, and '67).

When you talk about batting averages and who really was the best hitter in baseball, all attention is directed at Ted Williams. It's funny because Ted disliked—if not hated—the fans. So he had to have been pretty great to be so unpleasant and have us all still fawning over him. So we continue to fawn.

SEPTEMBER 28, 1941

Boston Red Sox left fielder Ted Williams started the last day of the season with a batting average of .39955. Williams decided against manager Joe Cronin's offer to sit out the day and have his average round up to .400. In the double-header in Philadelphia, Williams hit a home run and two singles in game one and a double and three singles in the nightcap to finish the season batting .4057 (.406).

SEPTEMBER 28, 1960

Ted Williams, at age 42, played his last major-league game. Williams, who had planned to retire at the season's end, retired three games early, skipping the final three games at Yankee Stadium. In the final at-bat of his career, Williams hit homer 521 in the eighth inning off Baltimore's Jack Fisher, when he turned on a 1–1 fastball and hit it out over the right-center-field bull pen. Bud Thomas allowed Williams's first career homer on April 23, 1939. He finished his 19-year career with a .344 lifetime batting average, won two triple crowns, hit 17 grand slams, and is the last player to hit .400 in a major-league season.

Who was on deck when Williams hit this homer? Catcher Jim Pagliaroni. After trotting out to left field in the ninth, Williams was immediately replaced by Carroll Hardy.

Williams, nicknamed the "Splendid Splinter," won six batting titles in his career. At age 42, he hit .316. In 1966, Frank Robinson won the American League batting title, hitting .316!

SEPTEMBER 28, 1930

Chicago Cubs center fielder Lewis "Hack" Wilson had two runs batted in in the season's final game to set a major-league record of 190 runs batted in in a season. The previous day, Wilson had slugged his fifty-fifth and fifty-sixth homers to set the National League record for home runs in a season. Roger Maris holds the major-league home run record with 61 in 1961.

SEPTEMBER 29, 1987

New York Yankee Don Mattingly, who started the season without ever having hit a grand slam, hit his sixth grand slam of the season, which set a major-league record. Four days before, Mattingly had connected for his fifth grand slam, tying him with the Chicago Cubs' Ernie Banks (1955) and the Baltimore Orioles' Jim Gentile (1961). In July of the same season, Mattingly homered in eight straight games to tie the major-league record for home runs in consecutive games set in 1956 by Pittsburgh's Dale Long. It was tied again by Ken Griffey, Jr., in 1995.

SEPTEMBER 7, 1974

Nolan Ryan of the California Angels hit the century mark. One of Ryan's pitches in a game against the Chicago White Sox was clocked at 100.8 mph, the first time in major-league history a pitch had ever been thrown over 100 mph.

SEPTEMBER 14, 1987

The Toronto Blue Jays hit a major-league-record ten home runs in their 18–3 victory over Baltimore. Ernie Whitt led the Blue Jays with three homers, while George Bell and Rance Mulliniks had two each. Fred McGriff, Lloyd Moseby, and Rob Ducey each had one. Cal and Billy Ripken were the first brother combination to be managed by a father in the majors.

SEPTEMBER 7, 1993

St. Louis Cardinal Mark Whiten tied Jim "Boom Boom" Bottomley's 1924 major-league record of 12 RBIs in one game. Whiten hit four homers, tying the major-league mark, in the second game of a doubleheader against Cincinnati. He had one RBI in the first game of the doubleheader to tie Nate Colbert's 1972 record of 13 RBIs in a doubleheader. Whiten had misplayed a ball in game one to allow the Reds to win, 14–13.

SEPTEMBER 14, 1990

Although this happened in September, you can use it anytime. Maybe on Father's Day. Seattle's Ken Griffey, Sr., connected on an 0–2 pitch and hit a home run over the center-field fence in the first inning. The pitcher was California Angel Kirk McCaskill, who took a deep breath and faced his next batter, Ken Griffey, Jr., who hit a 3–0 pitch over the center-field fence for a home run for the first father-son back-to-back home runs.

OBNOXIOUS POINT
Ken Griffey, Jr., was born in Donora, Pennsylvania, the birthplace of another great hitter, Stan "The Man" Musial.

ANOTHER OBNOXIOUS POINT
Musial had 3,630 lifetime hits.
1,815 on the road. 1,815 at home.
Consistency.

**People turn 40 all the time. And these days,
with training habits light-years better
than they were in the "old days," there is
a sprinkling of athletes who are 40 or more
and still contributing.**

SEPTEMBER 24, 1992

Forty-year-old Toronto Blue Jay Dave Winfield became the oldest major leaguer ever to register 100 RBIs in one season. He hit his twenty-third homer and had four RBIs in a win over the Orioles 8–2 to bring his season RBI total to 103.

SEPTEMBER 25, 1965

Satchel Paige, the oldest player in major-league history at an estimated 59 years, 8 months, and 5 days, pitched the last game of his career. He threw three scoreless innings, giving up only one hit, to Carl Yastrzemski.

These days it's a big deal to see a two-sport player. Bo Jackson played baseball and football for a while. So did Deion Sanders. (Go back to April and see Deion.) But rarely do you see an athlete move around in the same sport, from, say, first base one day to third the next. We live in an era of specialty players. You pick a position. You get good at it. You stay there. Given this, impress your friends with Bert Campaneris.

SEPTEMBER 8, 1965

The Oakland A's Bert Campaneris became the first player in major-league history to play all nine positions in the same game. He was forced to leave the game, which the California Angels won 5–3 in 13 innings, after 8⅔ innings because of a collision with catcher Ed Kirkpatrick.

SEPTEMBER 22, 1968

Minnesota's Cesar Tovar tied Bert Campaneris's 1965 record of most positions played in a major-league game. Tovar played all nine positions against the Oakland Athletics. As the starting pitcher, the first batter he faced was Campaneris, who fouled out. The second batter, Reggie Jackson, struck out. Tovar, normally a shortstop, had one hit and scored one run in the Twins' 2–1 win.

ARGUMENT STARTER
Should Pete Rose be allowed into the
Baseball Hall of Fame? The answer is
yes. The answer is that he bet
on baseball, so he should have been
banned from the game. The real
argument winner happened in
September.

SEPTEMBER 11, 1985

Cincinnati Red Pete Rose singled off San Diego's Eric Show for his major-league record of 4,192 hits. Rose broke the record of Ty Cobb, who had played his last game 57 years ago to the day. Rose's 15-year-old son, Petey, led the charge of teammates onto the field to congratulate the 44-year-old Rose. Reds owner Marge Schott gave Rose a red Corvette that had the license plate PR 4192 as a gift.

SPEAKING OF BANNED FROM BASEBALL:
When you hear of any sports scandal, it's still hard
to beat this one.

SEPTEMBER 28, 1920

Eight members of the 1919 Chicago White Sox were indicted by a grand jury in Chicago on charges that they conspired to fix the 1919 World Series and allowed the Cincinnati Reds to win. White Sox owner Charles Comiskey immediately suspended the eight, including "Shoeless" Joe Jackson. The players were acquitted, but they were banned from baseball for life.

You're watching a doubleheader . . .

SEPTEMBER 3, 1917

Philadelphia Phillies pitcher Grover Cleveland Alexander recorded complete-game wins in both ends of a doubleheader with the Brooklyn Dodgers. He allowed a major-league-record-tying one walk in a doubleheader.

Somebody says so-and-so is a pioneer. Or he is a role model. Or he has integrity. Nobody matches Arthur Ashe, who died of complications from AIDS in 1993. He was a great, great man.

SEPTEMBER 9, 1968

Twenty-five-year-old amateur Arthur Ashe won the first-ever U.S. Open men's singles title and became the first African-American to win a men's singles title in a Grand Slam tournament. Because he was not a professional at the time, Ashe was ineligible to accept the $14,000 first prize and instead received $280 for expenses incurred over the two-week period from the tournament's $20 per diem rate.

Before he died, he wrote the following to his daughter, Camera: "Along the way you will stumble, and perhaps even fall, but that, too, is normal and to be expected. Get up, get back on your feet, chastened but wiser, and continue on down the road.

"I may not be walking with you, all the way, or even much of the way, as I walk with you now. Don't be angry with me if I am not there in person, alive and well, when you need me. Do not feel sorry for me if I am gone. When we were together, I loved you deeply and you gave me so much happiness I can never repay you. Camera, wherever I am when you feel sick at heart and weary of life, or when you stumble and fall and don't know if you can get up again, think of me. I will be watching and smiling and cheering you on." This quote tells you more about Arthur Ashe than anything he did with a racket.

Other tennis news pales, but there's been some great stuff in September because this is the month of the U.S. Open, now played at Arthur Ashe Stadium in Flushing Meadows, New York. In between the $6 hamburgers and the $50 T-shirts is some memorable tennis.

SEPTEMBER 7, 1980

Twenty-one-year-old John McEnroe staved off Björn Borg and his attempt at a third straight come-from-behind victory in the tournament in five sets. McEnroe won 7–6, 6–1, 6–7, 5–7, 6–4 for his second men's singles title in a row. Borg had been down two sets to love against Johan Kriek in the semifinals and two sets to one in the quarter finals against Roscoe Tanner.

SEPTEMBER 8, 1984

Known as one of the single greatest days in tennis history. Play began at 11:07 A.M. and did not conclude until 11:14 P.M. All four stadium court matches were played to the maximum number of sets: Stan Smith beat John Newcombe 4–6, 7–5, 6–2 in the senior men's semifinals; Ivan Lendl defeated Pat Cash 3–6, 6–3, 6–4, 6–7, 7–6, including a saving match point in the first men's semifinals; Martina Navratilova won her second consecutive singles title over Chris Evert Lloyd 4–6, 6–4, 6–4; and, finally, John McEnroe overtook two-time defending champion Jimmy Connors 6–4, 4–6, 7–5, 4–6, 6–3.

SEPTEMBER 9, 1990

Unheralded Pete Sampras fired 13 aces in his 6–4, 6–3, 6–2 rout over André Agassi just 28 days after his nineteenth birthday and went into the record books as the youngest U.S. Open men's singles champion, replacing Oliver Campbell, who was 19 years, 6 months old when he won the U.S. Open in 1890. Sampras went on to win the U.S. Open singles title in 1993, 1995, and 1996.

SEPTEMBER 8, 1979

At age 16 years, 8 months, and 28 days, Tracy Austin became the youngest woman to win the U.S. Open when she upset Chris Evert Lloyd, snapping Lloyd's 31-match U.S. Open win streak. Austin won the U.S. Open a second time in 1981 by beating Martina Navratilova. Navratilova, in her first U.S. Open final, double-faulted the match away on the last point in the final set tiebreaker.

SEPTEMBER 8, 1969

Australian Rod Laver won the U.S. Open to complete his second Grand Slam. In a strategic move, Laver switched from sneakers to spikes after losing the first set. The tennis Grand Slam, consisting of the Australian, French, and U.S. opens, and Wimbledon, has only been won nine times in either singles or doubles. Only two players have done it twice: Laver (1962 singles, 1969 singles) and Margaret Smith Court (1970 singles, 1963 doubles).

I hate to say this, but we've come a long way, baby. Doesn't it sound a little strange now? In this age of Ellen DeGeneres and Madonna, and the WNBA, it seems silly when we recall where our heads were in September 1973 when Billie Jean King defeated Bobby Riggs in the "Battle of the Sexes" at Houston's Astrodome. Over 30,000 spectators witnessed King, age 29, and Riggs, age 55, settle the debate.

Although the tennis was awful, King's victory was a win for the women's movement. King vomited in the locker room before the match, then settled down to win 6–4, 6–3, 6–3. Before her victory, King stated that "women were chokers and spastics who couldn't take pressure. Except, of course, in childbirth."

SEPTEMBER 23, 1992

Goalie Manon Rheaume became the first woman to play in a National Hockey League game when her team, the Tampa Bay Lightning, met the St. Louis Blues in an exhibition match. The 20-year-old Rheaume played one period and registered seven saves.

SEPTEMBER 5, 1979

Ann Meyers, an All-American basketball player from UCLA, made history by becoming the first woman to sign a professional basketball contract, with the Indiana Pacers of the NBA. Meyers worked out with the team throughout training camp but was cut before the season started.

There is some basketball news in September. Big news.

SEPTEMBER 12, 1984

The Chicago Bulls signed their number one draft choice, Michael Jordan, from North Carolina. Jordan was selected third behind Akeem (later Hakeem) Olajuwon, who was taken by Houston, and Sam Bowie, who was drafted by Portland. With their tenth-round pick, the Bulls selected Carl Lewis.

SEPTEMBER 13, 1970

Try this one on marathon Sunday in New York. As you watch the stream of 25,000 or so run through the streets of New York City, remind your friends of the very first NYC Marathon, on September 13, 1970, which drew 126 runners. Only 55 people actually finished. Gary Muhrcke won with a time of 2:31:38.2.

You're watching a Pay-Per-View match with two overweight guys who aren't hitting each other, or if they are it's below the belt. You remember back to the time when life around the boxing world was a tad more glamorous.

SEPTEMBER 1, 1923

Birthday of Rocky Marciano, born Rocco Francis Marchigiano, known for attempts to batter opponents into insensibility as fast as possible. Marciano almost died from pneumonia as a child. In his youth, his favorite sport was baseball, not boxing. Marciano fought Jersey Joe Walcott for the heavyweight title on September 23, 1952, and knocked him out. In 1956, he retired as undefeated champion.

SEPTEMBER 15, 1978

Muhammad Ali, then known as Cassius Clay, became the first fighter to win the heavyweight championship for a third time with a unanimous 15-round decision over Leon Spinks. He won his first title on February 25, 1964, beating Sonny Liston. He regained the title the first time on October 30, 1974, by knocking out George Foreman.

You have your pick in September of two great Olympic stories, both memorable for different reasons.

SEPTEMBER 4, 1972

United States swimmer Mark Spitz won his seventh gold medal at the 1972 Olympic Games in Munich by swimming the butterfly leg on the gold medal–winning U.S. 4 × 100-meter medley relay team. Amazingly, all seven of Spitz's gold-medal performances set world records. Spitz also won golds in the 200-meter freestyle, 4 × 100-meter freestyle, 200-meter butterfly, 100-meter butterfly, 4 × 200-meter relay team as the anchor, and 100-meter freestyle. No other Olympic athlete has ever won seven gold medals in a single Olympic Games.

SEPTEMBER 5–6, 1972

Eleven members of the Israeli Olympic team were killed in an attempted kidnapping and attack on the Olympic Village in Munich. Four of seven guerrillas, members of the Black September faction of the Palestinian Liberation Army, were also killed. The most chilling words I think I've ever heard in television sports came from Jim McKay, the ABC host who, when he found out the athletes were murdered, said: "They're all gone."

You say Tiger Woods. I say Bobby Jones.

SEPTEMBER 27, 1930

Golfer Bobby Jones won the U.S. Amateur to become the only golfer ever to win a recognized Grand Slam, four major championships in a single season. Jones had already won the U.S. Open, British Open, and British Amateur. The current men's professional Grand Slam, the Masters, U.S. Open, British Open, and PGA championship, did not gain acceptance until 30 years later, when Arnold Palmer won the 1960 Masters and U.S. Open. Jones founded the Masters tournament in 1934.

SEPTEMBER 3, 1990

Chicago White Sox pitcher Bobby Thigpen set a major-league record with his forty-seventh save of the season. He finished the year with 57 saves in 65 opportunities. Win 57 came on September 30 in the last game of the season played at Comiskey Park. Thigpen had been an outfielder in his college days at Mississippi State.

SEPTEMBER 22, 1990

Illinois fullback Howard Griffith scored a record eight touchdowns as Illinois beat Southern Illinois, 56–21. Griffith scored on three straight carries in the second quarter. He also set the record for most points scored in a major college game: 48.

DREAM TEAM II
FOOTBALL

You could probably get by with the '85 Bears or the 49ers teams of the eighties or that perfect Dolphin team of 1972 as your best football team ever, but it's more fun to mix the players up. Don't let anyone argue with you.

BACKS AND RECEIVERS

RUNNING BACK: Walter Payton. Here's a simple fact to remember: the NFL's all-time leading rusher with 16,726 yards. Nine pro bowls. Ran for 275 yards in one game! He ran behind Jackie Slater and also found the time to throw eight touchdown passes for the Chicago Bears.

QUARTERBACK: Joe Montana. Three-time Super Bowl MVP. Four Super Bowl rings. The man. He was a third-round pick in 1979—81 players were picked ahead of him—but here he is *your* quarterback. Little-known fact: Joe was visiting South Bend, Indiana, to look at the Notre Dame football program and was in the stands in January of 1974 when Notre Dame's basketball team snapped UCLA's 88-game winning streak.

WIDE RECEIVER: Jerry Rice. Again, one of those players whose potential was not seen by the draft gods. Was the third wideout drafted in 1985, taken sixteenth overall by the 49ers. But, oh, is this guy the greatest. Look in the record books and see that his name is next to virtually every key receiving stat in NFL history. MVP of Super Bowl XXIII in 1989. Caught 11 passes for a record 215 yards. (Your quarterback threw them.)

OFFENSIVE LINE

GUARD: John Hannah. New England, *the man* at this position. Ten-time all pro. Hall of Famer.

TACKLE: Art Shell. Oakland. Played in three decades. Eight pro bowls, 23 postseason games. Hall of Famer.

CENTER: Dwight Stephenson. Miami. Big, tough, seamless.

DEFENSE

DEFENSIVE END: David "Deacon" Jones. He played mostly for the Rams and is the man who came up with the word "sack" for smashing a quarterback to the ground before he can throw the ball. He's also the NFL's all-time sack leader.

LINEBACKER: Lawrence Taylor. New York Giants. Player of the Year in 1986. Somebody says Ray Nitschke? Dick Butkus? Don't even look at them. Four times Taylor had 15 or more sacks in a season, including 20 in 1986. Ten pro bowls. Unlike Ray and Dick, Lawrence was a franchise player.

DEFENSIVE BACK: Herb Adderley. Former Green Bay and Dallas great. Played in four Super Bowls and five pro bowls and had 48 career interceptions.

DB: Ronnie Lott. Nobody could hit like that guy. Nine pro bowls. Just keep saying "Nobody could hit like that guy."

COACH

Got a problem here. You can't decide. On a Monday, you're going to go with the Steelers' Chuck Noll, the only coach to win four Super Bowls. On Tuesday, Tom Landry, the legendary coach of the Dallas Cowboys. On Wednesday, Bill Walsh, the genius of the 49ers and inventor of the West Coast Offense. On Thursday, Don Shula, the NFL's all-time winningest coach. On Friday, go with "Papa Bear" George Halas: 40 seasons. 7 NFL titles. 324 games. On Saturday, Joe Gibbs of the Washington Redskins, who had three Super Bowl wins. But on Sunday, when it counts, let's shout it together: Vince Lombardi of Green Bay, who won Super Bowls I and II. Lombardi was the first to utter these words: "Winners never quit. Quitters never win."

Just as January is football and March is college basketball and June is the NBA Finals, make no mistake about this: October is baseball. And there is nothing like it. It is the time of the year when every pitch, every swing, counts. Every game is an event. It is the time of year when the World Series, emotionally known as the "Fall Classic," is played. It is no wonder that Tommy Lasorda, the man who came up with the phrase, managed in four World Series and won two of them. Let's say you end up in the same gym or Italian restaurant with the skipper and *bang!* he's talkin' baseball and you're listening. Suddenly you're talking, and you begin by asking him about the night of October 15, 1988, Los Angeles Dodgers hosting the Oakland Athletics at Dodger Stadium. Game 1.

Los Angeles is down to its last out and trailing 4–3 with former A's outfielder Mike Davis on base on a walk by the great reliever Dennis Eckersley. At this point in the game, Lasorda's bench is gone. He's already gone through four pinch hitters. Tommy's got a decision to make. He wonders if Kirk Gibson, who is limping around in the tunnel because of a leg injury, has enough in him for a history-making at-bat. He puts him in, and Gibson battles with Eckersley, and suddenly it's a full count. The crowd is on its feet. Los Angeles is glued to the television. The next pitch—a slider—Gibson whacks toward the right-field fence. As soon as it leaves the bat, there's no question it's a home run. Jack Buck says on the radio: "I don't believe what I just saw." Neither did anybody else. It was a scene out of Bernard Malamud's novel *The Natural.* Gibson rounded the bases pumping his arm and smiling, and as he touched home plate, he completed one of the most famous World Series home runs ever. Oakland never recovered, and the Dodgers won in five.

Everybody loves home runs. Everybody loves dramatic home run stories. Which one was more dramatic? Let your friends decide.

OCTOBER 1, 1932

At Wrigley Field in Chicago, Yankee slugger Babe Ruth made a sweeping gesture toward the center-field stands, then hit Charlie Root's 2–2 pitch right where he had pointed. It was Ruth's second homer of the game, and it broke a 4–4 tie in Game 3 of the World Series. Many debate whether Ruth really called the home run, but it certainly adds to the Babe's legend. New York won the game 7–5 and the World Series in a four-game sweep.

OCTOBER 3, 1951

New York Giants third baseman Bobby Thomson hit the "shot heard 'round the world." His three-run, ninth-inning homer gave the Giants a 5–4 win over Brooklyn in the decisive third game of a National League pennant play-off. New York was down 4–2 with two outs but plated four in the ninth to win it. The pitcher who gave up Thomson's shot? Ralph Branca. Thomson was the only batter he faced!

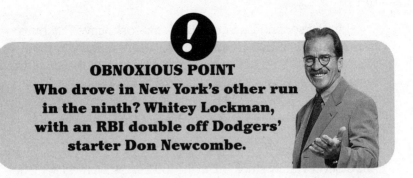

OBNOXIOUS POINT
Who drove in New York's other run
in the ninth? Whitey Lockman,
with an RBI double off Dodgers'
starter Don Newcombe.

The game was played before 34,320 at the Polo Grounds. How many more fans claim they were there? Brooklyn manager Chuck Dressen was second-guessed for not walking Thomson with first base open. As late as August 11 of that season, New York trailed Brooklyn by 13 games. The Giants, aided by a 16-game winning streak late in the season, then caught the Dodgers.

Branca's uniform number? 13.

Who will ever forget Russ Hodges's call "The Giants win the pennant, the Giants win the pennant!" as bedlam reigned at the Polo Grounds. Hodges's call is probably the most famous in baseball history. Because it was a weekday afternoon game, there were over 20,000 empty seats at the Polo Grounds. Willie Mays was on deck when Thomson homered.

OCTOBER 13, 1960

If you were to ask your friends who won the 1960 World Series and gave them this hint—the New York Yankees outscored the Pittsburgh Pirates 55–27 over the seven games, including a 16–3 Game 2 win, a 10–0 Game 3 triumph, and a Game 6 12–0 whitewashing, what team do you think they'd guess? The Yankees? *Wrong!*

Pirates second baseman Bill Mazeroski gave Pittsburgh its first World Series triumph in 35 years as he slugged a game-winning solo home run in the bottom of the ninth off Yankee reliever Ralph Terry, who lost both of his decisions in the 1960 Fall Classic. "Maz," the pride of Wheeling, West Virginia, was more known for his great glove than his stick. A seven-time National League All-Star, Mazeroski won eight Gold Glove Awards in recognition of his fielding prowess. But Maz's bat certainly stuck out in the '60 Series. Named MVP, he hit .320 with two homers and five RBIs versus the Yankees. Mazeroski's homer won the World Series. Thirty-three years later, north of the border, Toronto's Joe Carter went into the history books by hitting a Game 6, bottom-of-the-ninth, World Series–winning three-run homer off Philadelphia closer Mitch "Wild Thing" Williams.

OCTOBER 18, 1977

Yankee slugger Reggie Jackson became "Mr. October" as he hit three home runs against L.A. in Game 6 of the '77 World Series. New York won the Series 4–2, and Jackson set a Series record with five homers, each of which he hit on the first pitch. The hurlers? Burt Hooton, Elias Sosa, and Charlie Hough. Babe Ruth is the only other player to homer three times in a World Series game. He did it twice. Although it was New York's twenty-first World Series title, it was the Yankees' first since 1962. For Jackson, four of the homers came on four swings. He had homered in his last at-bat of Game 5, so he hit four home runs in four consecutive official at-bats (he walked once) on four pitches.

OCTOBER 2, 1978

Bucky Dent hit a three-run homer in the top of the seventh inning off Boston's Mike Torrez, sparking New York to a 5–4 win at Fenway Park in a one-game play-off for the American League East Division title. New York had come back from a 14-game deficit at midseason. The Yankees also trailed 2–0 in this game!

Red Sox great Carl Yastrzemski made the last out of the game with the tying run on third base. Dent had hit just five home runs that season. Better known as a solid defensive shortstop, Dent led American League shortstops in fielding three times. Looks like the Curse of the Bambino lives on in Beantown. Dent went on to win World Series MVP as New York overcame an 0–2 deficit to beat L.A. in six games.

Anytime you can invoke Ebbets Field in Brooklyn, you not only sound good, you are good.

OCTOBER 3, 1947

At Ebbets Field, Yankees pitcher Bill Bevens allowed a two-out, two-run double to Dodgers pinch-hitter Cookie Lavagetto in the ninth inning. Why is this a big deal? Because Bevens had surrendered no hits up to that juncture and was trying to become the first-ever pitcher to throw a no-hitter in World Series play. After Bevens issued his ninth and tenth walks of the game, Lavagetto hit an opposite-field two-bagger, giving Brooklyn the Game 4, 3–2 win and Bevens a lot of heartache. New York ultimately won this dramatic series four games to three over its dreaded rivals. Bevens's ten walks in a World Series game is still a single-game record!

Bobby Thomson's "shot heard 'round the world" was hit four years to the day after Bill Bevens's near no-no. Something about October 3? you wonder.

Greatest home run ever?
Or certainly the most talked about.

OCTOBER 1, 1961

New York outfielder Roger Maris hit his sixty-first home run of the season at Yankee Stadium, breaking Babe Ruth's 1927 record of 60. Boston right-hander Tracy Stallard gave up the record-breaking homer in the fourth inning. Ruth hit 59 "dingers" in 1921. In 1927, he hit 60 in 540 at-bats in a 154-game season. In 1961, in a 162-game schedule, Maris hit 61 in 590 at-bats. A 19-year-old truck driver from Coney Island, Sal Durante, caught Maris's home run ball in Box 163D in section 33 of Yankee Stadium. Durante got $5,000 from Sam Gordon, a Sacramento, California, restaurant owner who had publicly offered that amount for the ball. Maris's homer accounted for the only run in the game.

You're watching a young pitcher at work out there, and people all around you are marveling at his poise. So you bring up . . .

OCTOBER 6, 1966

Jim Palmer of the Baltimore Orioles became the youngest-ever pitcher to hurl a World Series shutout, beating the Dodgers 6–0 on a four-hitter. Palmer was 20 years, 11 months, and 21 days old. L.A. committed six errors. For L.A., it was losing pitcher Sandy Koufax's last big-league appearance. A three-time Cy Young Award winner, Koufax announced his retirement on November 18, 1966, at the age of 30 because of an arthritic elbow. Palmer's win in Game 2 gave the O's a 2–0 lead, and they swept L.A. 4–0. Palmer also ended his career with three Cy Young trophies. He also had victories in the 1970, 1971, and 1983 World Series. He's the only pitcher in major-league history to win a World Series game in each of three decades. A great high school athlete in Arizona, Palmer was the three-sport, all-state honoree. John Wooden offered him a basketball scholarship to come to UCLA.

In over 4,000 career innings, Palmer never allowed a grand slam in the big leagues. Johnny Bench did hit one off him in the minor leagues in 1967, when Palmer was at Rochester for a brief stint. Palmer's final career win was in Game 3 of the '83 World Series against Philadelphia.

Palmer's nickname was "Cakes" because he won seven of eight starts at one point in 1966 after eating pancakes for breakfast. Thus, pancakes became a staple on Palmer's menu on the day he pitched.

No matter where you go, everybody loves a good New York Mets story. You can go with their 120 losses in 1962; you can go with the Amazin' Mets in 1969 behind Tom Seaver as they beat the Cubs in a dramatic down-the-stretch pennant race. But here's a significant Mets story you can matter-of-factly toss out.

OCTOBER 8, 1991

Junior Noboa was acquired by the New York Mets on waivers from the Montreal Expos. Why is this interesting? Because the Mets have used over 100 different third basemen since their inception in 1962. Noboa is one of those 100-plus, and, in his only chance, while playing third for the Mets, he committed an error. Speaking of the number one, Noboa was born on the eleventh (2 ones) month of the year, and he hit just one career homer in his brief stay in the big leagues. That came on May 24, 1991, off the Cubs' Paul Assenmacher.

Don Zimmer was the first-ever player to man third base for the Mets. Speaking of Juniors besides Cal Ripken and Ken Griffey, how about Toronto's Junior Felix? On May 4, 1989, he became the eleventh major leaguer to homer on the first major-league pitch thrown to him. The victim? California's Kirk McCaskill.

The high five. You've used it when your kid gets an A on his math test. You high-five your husband or wife when he or she does something great at the office. Your promotion comes through? You high-five an office mate. Great sermon, Father? High five. Your office basketball team beats the suits. High fives all over the place. Some people even high-five themselves.

Who invented the high five? Well, there's some dispute, but we think that it happened on October 5.

OCTOBER 5, 1977

It's appropriate that on October 5, the first high five, between Los Angeles Dodgers Glenn Burke and Dusty Baker, was recorded. Some people claim the high five existed before this. Baker had just hit a grand slam off Phillies pitcher Jim Lonborg, snapping a 1–1 tie in the bottom of the fourth inning at Dodger Stadium. As Baker entered the dugout, Burke came out to greet him and wound up his arm in a motion spontaneously matched by Baker. Some claim that the high five has existed in women's volleyball since at least 1970.

There is some school of thought that Magic Johnson invented the high five at Michigan State or that Dave Stewart might have had a hand in this, but I'd go with Dusty and Glenn.

George Steinbrenner once called Dave Winfield "Mr. May" because, he said, he couldn't get it done in October. In the '81 World Series with the Yankees and Dodgers Winfield went 1 for 22. But Winfield, who was born in October, won a World Series in October with Toronto. Not getting it done?

OCTOBER 3, 1951

Winfield was born in St. Paul, Minnesota, on the same day Bobby Thomson hit "the shot heard 'round the world." Winfield is unique because he was the first to bypass minor-league baseball and immediately joined the San Diego Padres upon leaving the University of Minnesota, where he also played basketball. In college, Winfield was a great pitcher, going 9–1, with 109 strikeouts in 82 innings in the spring of '73. He made his big-league debut on June 19, 1973. Winfield, who finished his career with 3,110 hits, was also drafted in 1973 in the seventeenth round as a tight end by his hometown Vikings, in the sixth round by the ABA's Utah Stars, and in the fifth round by the NBA's Atlanta Hawks. Atlanta's fourth-round pick that year? Fox Sports's James Brown, who played at Harvard. Neither Brown nor Winfield ever played with the Hawks. Winfield holds the career record for doubles in All-Star Game competition with seven.

OCTOBER 18, 1964

 Swimmer Don Schollander of Lake Oswego, Oregon, became the first American to win four Olympic gold medals since Jesse Owens in 1936. The U.S. won 36 gold medals at the '64 games in Tokyo. Joe Frazier won a gold in heavyweight boxing, and "Bullet Bob" Hayes captured a gold in the 100-meter dash. Tokyo was the first Asian city to host the games. Frazier, with a broken right hand, still beat Germany's Hans Hube. Al Oerter won his third straight gold in the discus.

You think we finished with hockey in June. It's back. Hockey, seemingly, is played year-round, but in October there are some especially memorable moments.

OCTOBER 5, 1965

Patrick Roy (pronounced "Wah") was born in Quebec City, Quebec. A goaltender, Roy led the Montreal Canadiens to a Stanley Cup win in 1986 and as a 20-year-old became the youngest player ever to capture the Conn Smythe Trophy as finals MVP in the play-offs. Roy had a 15–5 play-off record that season and allowed just 1.92 goals per game in those 20 outings. The Stanley Cup win over Calgary also gave Montreal its twenty-third championship, a new professional record for most championship seasons. The Canadiens had been tied with baseball's New York Yankees at 22. On April 24, 1997, Roy set an NHL record with his eighty-ninth career play-off victory, surpassing former New York Islanders goalie Billy Smith, who had 88. Roy shut out Chicago 7–0 for the record-breaking win. It was Roy's tenth career play-off shutout.

OCTOBER 11, 1984

Pittsburgh Penguins center rookie Mario Lemieux, age 19, scored his first career goal in his first game in the NHL on his first shift on his first shot at Boston. Lemieux stole the puck from Bruins defenseman Ray Bourque and bore down on goaltender Pete Peeters, beating him with a backhand shot. Lemieux had picked number 66 for his jersey number because it was Wayne Gretzky's number upside down! Lemieux would go on to score more than 600 goals in his 13-year career. He won six scoring titles, three All-Star Game MVP awards, and two play-off MVP awards and scored five goals in a game four times. He led Pittsburgh to back-to-back Stanley Cup wins in 1991 and 1992. New York Rangers goaltender John Vanbiesbrouck was victimized 30 times by Lemieux. No goalie allowed Mario more goals than that. He's the only player in NHL history to have won the Calder, Hart, Ross, Smythe, and Masterton trophies.

OCTOBER 16, 1946

Gordie Howe of the Detroit Red Wings scored his first career goal against Toronto goaltender Turk Broda. Eighteen years later, Howe would score goal 545 to become the league's all-time goals-scored leader. Howe would go on to play an NHL-record 26 seasons with Detroit and Hartford. He played in 1,767 NHL games, scoring a total of 801 goals in regular-season play. He also assisted on 1,049 regular season goals. After leaving Detroit in 1971, he played in the WHA, then came back in 1979 for one final NHL season with Hartford. He helped lead Detroit to four Stanley Cups. He played with his sons, Mark and Marty, on the 1979–80 Hartford team. His number 9 jersey has been retired by the Detroit Red Wings. He was inducted into the Hockey Hall of Fame in 1972. He appeared in 23 NHL All-Star Games. He won six Hart Trophies, as the league's MVP. Howe played in five decades (the forties through the eighties). "Power" became Howe's nickname because he literally powered his way through the players from the blue line to the goalmouth. Howe was a grandfather of two when he played for Hartford.

You've already learned how to drop in Joe DiMaggio's 56-game hitting streak and Wilt Chamberlain's 100-point game when you are talking about records. But not many people think of Bob Beamon right off the bat. Except you, of course.

OCTOBER 18, 1968

At the 1968 Olympics in Mexico City, American Bob Beamon shattered the world record in the long jump by almost two feet. Beamon's gold medal–winning jump was 29′2½″! Did the high altitude (7,350 feet) assist Beamon? Beamon's best jump before this? A wind-aided 27′6″. Beamon, 22, was from Jamaica, Queens, in New York City.

The Mexico City jump was so astounding, officials thought the tape measure was broken and called for another. Beamon used to carry his gold medal around and let people touch it. So many people put their hands on it, the gold plating came off and the medal looked silver. So if somebody says he saw Beamon's medal and it *was* silver, set him straight.

OBNOXIOUS POINT

The Phoenix Suns drafted Bob Beamon in the fifteenth round of the 1969 NBA draft. The first overall pick that year? UCLA's Lew Alcindor, by Milwaukee. Phoenix took Neal Walk second that year. The Suns had lost the coin flip with Milwaukee for the right to pick first in that year's draft. P.S. Phoenix called heads on the coin toss.

OCTOBER 5, 1996

Dante Brown, a junior tailback from Orange Park, Florida, and a star at Division III Marietta (Ohio) College, set an NCAA All-Division record for rushing yards in a game with 441 yards on 45 carries and 6 touchdowns in a 43–30 win over Baldwin-Wallace. Carey Bender of Coe College set the previous mark of 417 yards in 1993.

OCTOBER 13, 1962

Jerry Lee Rice was born in Starkville, Mississippi. He was the first overall pick in the 1985 USFL draft by the Birmingham Stallions. He was also drafted by the San Francisco 49ers in the 1985 NFL draft as sixteenth overall pick, and he signed with the 49ers. Rice, as a junior, caught 24 passes in one game for Mississippi Valley State in Itta Bena and left school with 18 NCAA I-AA records. Archie "Gunslinger" Cooley was his coach, Willie "Satellite" Totten was his quarterback, and they ran the "Satellite Express" offense. Until 1997, Rice had never missed a game in college or in the NFL. Rice's dad, Joe Nathan, was a bricklayer. As a teenager, Jerry, his dad, and his brothers worked eight-hour shifts in the summer sun hoisting mortar and catching the bricks tossed up to them on the scaffold in Mississippi. Coach Cooley once told me Rice was so good he could catch a BB in the dark. He can also slam-dunk a basketball.

OCTOBER 8, 1956

In Game 5 of the '56 World Series, New York Yankees right-hander Don Larsen hurled the only perfect game in World Series history. It came at the expense of the Brooklyn Dodgers. Dale Mitchell made the last out of the game on a called third strike. Final score: New York 2, Brooklyn 0. A perfect game takes place when a pitcher faces 27 batters (9 innings × 3 batters) and not one reaches first base through a hit, base on balls (walk), error, or any other means. Larsen went to ball three on just one batter, Pee Wee Reese. New York won the series four games to three.

OBNOXIOUS POINT
First subway series 1921 New York Yankees versus New York Giants. Giants won it in eight games (yes, eight).

DREAM TEAM III
BASKETBALL

CENTER

Some of the best arguments in sports revolve around an all-time basketball dream team. It begins, always, at center. There's a group that goes with Wilt Chamberlain, simply for the offensive numbers he put up and his rebounding, which has been equaled nowhere. Chamberlain holds 56 regular-season records. Think about this: He scored 50 or more points in a game 45 times in the 1961–62 season. That was the season in which he *averaged* 50.4 points a game and 25.7 rebounds. Wilt used to dunk from the free-throw line.

Wilt's only drawback: He won only two NBA championship rings. We say "only" because Kareem Abdul-Jabbar has six NBA championship rings and three college championships at UCLA. He is the NBA's all-time leading scorer with 38,387 points. The big guy played 20 seasons, won the MVP 6 times, and had the greatest jazz record collection ever until it burned down with his house. But many go with Bill Russell, as he had two NCAA championships of his own at San Francisco, a gold medal in the 1956 Olympics, and—get this—11 NBA titles.

GUARD

At guard, people get hysterical.

The old-timers always swoon at the thought of Bob Cousy, the Boston Celtic with six championship rings. It's safe to say Cousy invented modern-day passing and taught a generation about court vision. Think pass, not shot, was his mantra. Play-off consistency was his thing: In 109 play-off contests he averaged 19 points, 9 assists, and 5 rebounds.

Many people will forget about Oscar Robertson as one of the all-time best, so to remind them, mention that the "Big O" *averaged* a triple double with 30.8 points, 12.5 rebounds, and 22.4 assists per game in the 1961–62 season. He was MVP in 1964 and Rookie of the Year in 1961. But he got only one ring.

That guy on the NBA logo with the basketball is Jerry West—that's how good he was. "Mr. Clutch," you can call him. He scored 20 or more points in 25 straight finals games. One of the best NBA executives to ever steal players from other teams.

Magic Johnson. Who was bigger? He invented "show-time." He invented the pass as a thing that puts people in their seats. He invented smiling. Not really, but you'd think so. He invented the great interview. He invented enthusiasm. Isiah Thomas tells the story of the first time he saw Magic in college. He and some buddies drove down to Michigan State to see this 6'10" guard, and all they could say was "He can *play,* too."

Magic came out of retirement in 1992 to win NBA All-Star Game MVP. What can you say? Who's better, Michael Jordan? "Babe Ruth of Basketball"? Come on. Don't even try.

FORWARD

You're gonna get big arguments here, too, as it comes down to who you leave out, Like Elgin Baylor, John Stockton, John Havlicek. But so good were Julius Erving and Larry Bird, there is no further conversation, you say. "Dr. J" had a game and class beyond description, and Larry was so good he was called "Larry Legend" *while* he was playing. One's a coach and one's a TV guy now, but they'll always be known as the guy who made the house calls and the guy who made the shots.

COACH

I would not hesitate to put Pat Riley in charge of this group. But in this age of the cigar as a social instrument, better go with the Celtics' Red Auerbach, who won nine titles and had the ability to spot talent beyond his peers. He drafted Bird when he was a junior at Indiana State. He had to wait a year but thought it was worth it. It was. Five teams passed on Larry.

November

In November, we are thankful for sports and for all the records and big plays and games we get to see. Well, maybe we didn't see any of them. But we can pretend. That's not really lying, it's just B.S.-ing.

So over the Thanksgiving table perhaps you can say this little prayer: "We thank you for this food and family, ours and theirs . . . And oh, by the way, thanks for Payton and the Chicago Bears."

NOVEMBER 20, 1977

Walter Payton of the Chicago Bears set an NFL record with 275 yards rushing in a 10–7 victory over the Minnesota Vikings at Soldier Field. Payton, a seven-time Pro Bowl selection and the NFL Player of the Year in 1977, is the NFL's all-time leading rusher, with 16,726 career yards.

You have Joe Montana, he has Johnny Unitas; back in the forties they had Sid Luckman.

NOVEMBER 14, 1943

Nineteen forty-three NFL MVP Sid Luckman of the Chicago Bears became the first professional quarterback to pass for more than 400 yards in a single game. Luckman completed 21 of 32 passes for 433 yards and 7 touchdowns en route to a 56–7 victory over the New York Giants. Luckman led the Bears to 4 NFL titles in his 12 seasons.

On Thanksgiving be thankful that you're healthy and in one piece. Then again, it's how you use your handicap that matters.

NOVEMBER 8, 1970

Tom Dempsey of the New Orleans Saints set an NFL record for the longest field goal. Trailing 17–16 with two seconds left to play, Dempsey hit a 63-yard field goal. The 6'1" 265-pound Dempsey was born without a right hand and with a club right foot that required a custom shoe for kicking.

On November 1 you can celebrate All Saints' Day and tell your sports buddies something they did not know.

NOVEMBER 1, 1966

On All Saints' Day, the NFL awarded a franchise to New Orleans. On January 9, 1967, the team was named the Saints and Tom Fears became its head coach. The Saints began play in the 1967 season. In their first game, rookie John Gilliam returned the opening kickoff 94 yards for a touchdown, but the Saints lost 27–13 to Los Angeles. Unfortunately for New Orleans, it wasn't until 1979 that the team finished a season without a losing record, going 8–8.

OBNOXIOUS POINT
Tom Fears of the Rams holds
the NFL record for most
receptions in a game with 18
versus the Packers in 1950.

**Hey, ever watch a game and they go to the
commercial early and you miss part of the
action? Or you're watching a celebration
at the end and somebody like me says,
"good night, everybody," and you're wondering why you didn't get to see the players celebrate or cry (or both)? How about
missing the entire end of a game that had
the comeback of the ages?**

NOVEMBER 17, 1968

NBC left a broadcast of a game between the Oakland
Raiders and the New York Jets with several minutes remaining on the clock in order to show the movie *Heidi* on
time. After *Heidi* started, the Raiders scored two touchdowns
in the final minutes for a 43–32 comeback win. Angry viewers
bombarded NBC with phone calls, leading to the current
process of delaying regular programming if games run long.

NOVEMBER 16, 1957

Notre Dame beat Oklahoma 7–0, ending the Sooners' 47-game college football winning streak. Who scored the lone touchdown of the game? Fighting Irish running back Dick Lynch. The Sooners were an 18-point favorite against Notre Dame. OU had routed Notre Dame 40–0 the season before. The last team to beat OU before this game? Notre Dame at the start of the '53 season. It was the first time in the last 124 games that OU was held scoreless.

And speaking of great finishes you did see. Was there ever a better college football game than Boston College/Miami in 1984? The answer is yes, but not on the night you tell this story.

NOVEMBER 23, 1984

Boston College quarterback Doug Flutie threw for 472 yards as the Eagles upset the Miami Hurricanes 47–45 in a game played at the Orange Bowl. BC won the game as Flutie completed a desperation 65-yard Hail Mary pass to Gerard Phelan for a touchdown.

NOVEMBER 20, 1982

The University of California football team beat Stanford 25–20 on the last play of the game. With Stanford leading 20–19, the Cardinals kicked off with only a few seconds left. The Cal players completed a series of five laterals in returning the kick for a touchdown. Besides avoiding the Stanford players, Cal had to maneuver around the Cardinal band, which had begun coming onto the field thinking the victory was secure.

It's election night and one of the political analysts brings up Ronald Reagan. You bring up Knute Rockne.

NOVEMBER 1, 1913

In the inaugural meeting between Notre Dame and Army, the forward pass was the difference. Notre Dame beat Army 35–13 by surprising the Cadets with a multitude of forward passes. Irish All-American quarterback Gus Dorais completed 14 of 17 passes for 243 yards. His main target was Knute Rockne. In another memorable meeting between the two teams, on November 8, 1946, Notre Dame tied Army 0–0 to snap West Point's 26-game winning streak.

NOVEMBER 26, 1976

The University of Pittsburgh's Tony Dorsett rushed for 220 yards to set an NCAA record for career rushing yards. In the process he became the first college football player to break 6,000 yards in rushing when he finished his career with

6,082 yards. He also had a record 33 games in which he gained 100 or more yards. As a senior, Dorsett led undefeated Pitt to the 1976 national title.

Nobody ever, ever said Tony Dorsett's name better during a football game than Pat Summerall. "DorSETT. Touchdown."

Baseball was without a commissioner for so long new fans to the game probably didn't know it needed one. Daddy, what's a commissioner?

NOVEMBER 12, 1920

Amid accusations that members of the Chicago White Sox conspired to fix the 1919 World Series, baseball owners appointed the game's first commissioner. Federal judge Kenesaw Mountain Landis replaced the three-man governing board called the National Commission. Landis cleaned up the game and restored baseball's integrity and America's confidence in its heroes. He served as commissioner until November 25, 1944.

NOVEMBER 6, 1861

Thankful there is basketball this month? Sing "Happy Birthday" on November 6, 1861, the birthdate of James Naismith, inventor of basketball at a Springfield, Massachusetts, YMCA as an indoor game to be played during the winter for exercise. A minister and a physical educator, he shunned competitive athletics and had little to do with the game he invented. He was inducted into the Hall of Fame as a charter member in 1959.

And Hall of Fame pitcher Walter Johnson was born this month, also on November 6. But this isn't the story, really. Just rattle off his Hall of Fame class and you're at the head of the class.

NOVEMBER 6, 1887

Johnson was nicknamed "The Big Train," indicating the respect other players gave his fastball. Johnson won 416 games in his major-league career, second in major-league history to Cy Young's 511. Johnson was a member of the 1936 first Hall of Fame class along with Ty Cobb, Christy Mathewson, Babe Ruth, and Honus Wagner. In voting by the Baseball Writers Association, Cy Young, Rogers Hornsby, Tris Speaker, and Napoleon Lajoie failed to be named on 75 percent of the ballots and were not elected. A separate vote was conducted for pre-1900 players, but no one was chosen.

NOVEMBER 21, 1956

Brooklyn Dodger pitcher Don Newcombe won the first Cy Young Award, given to the most outstanding pitcher in the major leagues. (From 1956 to 1966 only one award was given per year. Since 1967, a pitcher from each league has been selected.) Newcombe also won the National League MVP Award in 1956. Sandy Koufax (1963) and Bob Gibson (1968) are the only two other National League pitchers to win both awards in the same season.

NOVEMBER 19, 1979

Houston Astro Nolan Ryan signed a free agent contract with the California Angels and in the process became the first baseball free agent to sign a contract for a salary of $1,000,000 a year.

Think about what players make now and what a big deal this must have been in 1979. If you're an economics major or negotiator, you've got a couple hours of conversation here.

NOVEMBER 13, 1985

New York Met Dwight Gooden became the youngest pitcher ever to win the Cy Young Award. In his second year, Gooden finished 24–4 and led the majors with a 1.53 ERA and 268 strikeouts. (His 24 wins also led the majors in wins.)

"Dr. K" won the award three days short of his twenty-first birthday. On May 14, 1996, Gooden pitched a no-hitter for the Yankees as they beat the Seattle Mariners 2–0. Gooden's career was considered over by many after a drug ban the year before and a rough start to the 1996 season. Gooden struck out five and walked six in the no-hitter at Yankee Stadium.

Every now and then some front-office low-level marketing person will think of a promotion to get more fans in. In 1946, someone came up with a promo to keep them out.

NOVEMBER 1, 1946

The New York Knickerbockers and the Toronto Huskies met in the first Basketball Association of America official game. For this game, any fan taller than the Huskies 6'8" center George Nostrand was admitted free. The Knickerbockers emerged victorious, 68–66. The BAA merged with the National Basketball League in 1949 to form the National Basketball Association.

"No mas" **has been in the Hispanic vernacular since the beginning of time. But it took on new meaning on ...**

NOVEMBER 25, 1980

Sugar Ray Leonard regained the welterweight boxing title when Roberto Duran quit boxing with 16 seconds left in the eighth round, saying, *"No mas, no mas."* In 1976, Leonard, at age 21, won an Olympic gold medal for the U.S. He had fought with a picture of his three-year-old son, Ray, Jr., taped to his sneaker. Leonard was the first fighter to earn $100 million in purses and the first to win five titles in five divisions.

The seventies and eighties had Sugar Ray Leonard; the fifties and sixties had Floyd Patterson, who on November 30, 1956, won the heavyweight championship by knocking out Archie Moore in the fifth round of a fight in Chicago. Patterson won the title left vacant by Rocky Marciano, who retired as undefeated heavyweight champion on April 27.

NOVEMBER 22, 1986

Twenty-year-old Mike Tyson became the youngest heavyweight champion in history with his second-round knockout of Trevor Berbick for the World Boxing Council (WBC) heavyweight title.

Big paydays. Michael Jordan earns $30 million a year just *on* the court, right? Right. Tiger Woods walked into the game of golf with $60 million in endorsements. On November 9, 1996, Mike Tyson took home $30 million in a losing effort to Evander Holyfield at the MGM Grand in Las Vegas. Less than a minute into the eleventh round, Holyfield joined Muhammad Ali as the only three-time world heavyweight champion. He earned only $11 million. After the fight, Tyson said he was unable to remember anything from the third round on. I bet he remembered the $30 million, though.

You're watching a hockey game with friends and delighting in those colorful masks goalies wear. Let them talk about the goalie, you take the high road and talk about fashion.

NOVEMBER 1, 1959

Montreal Canadiens goaltender Jacques "Jake the Snake" Plante donned a mask against the Rangers after being hit in the face in the first period. His coach, Toe Blake, wasn't happy about the mask, but the Habs were in the midst of an 18-game unbeaten streak, so Blake calmed down and allowed Plante to keep the mask. He became the first goalie to use a mask regularly in games. Plante, as a member of five teams in his 18-season NHL career, was a member of six Stanley Cup–winning teams. He won five Vezina Trophies in a row as the NHL's top goalie and was inducted into the Hockey Hall of Fame in 1978. (He won a total of seven Vezina Trophies and was the league's MVP in 1962.) It's funny that the mask made its debut one day after Halloween.

Day you hated in November:

NOVEMBER 7, 1991

Earvin "Magic" Johnson retired from basketball after announcing that he had tested positive for HIV. He had discovered he was HIV positive after failing a routine insurance physical. After missing the first three games of the year, he stood at a podium at the Great Western Forum in Los Angeles and told the world. Despite his retirement, he played in the 1992 All-Star Game and was named MVP. Johnson played on the 1992 gold medal–winning U.S. Olympic team. He coached the Lakers for part of the 1993–94 season and briefly played during the 1995–96 season before going back into retirement.

December

Some of the best Christmas presents sports fans get are great football games in December. But let's get the college news out of the way first. The Heisman Trophy is awarded to the best—well, who the athletic departments' public relations guys are convinced is the best these days—football player in the country. Usually they are right. They were on . . .

DECEMBER 2, 1975

Ohio State running back Archie Griffin became the first and only collegiate player to win the Heisman Trophy two straight years. Griffin rushed for 5,177 yards on 845 carries for a remarkable 6.1 yards per attempt. Griffin was just 5'8" and weighed 184 pounds. California running back Chuck Muncie came in second in the voting in '75. The first winner, in 1935, was Chicago halfback Jay Berwanger. The trophy was originally named the DAC Trophy because the Downtown Athletic Club in New York City presented it. After John W. Heisman, an athletic director at the DAC, died in 1936, the trophy was renamed in his honor. Yale end Larry Kelley won the 1936 Heisman. Kelley and Notre Dame's Leon Hart, also an end, are the only two linemen to win the award. Hart won in 1949. No defensive player had ever won this award until Michigan's Charles Woodson won in 1997. Pitt defensive end Hugh Green had come close in 1980, finishing second to South Carolina running back George Rogers. Griffin is a member of the College Football Hall of Fame. He played seven seasons in the NFL, rushing for a total of 2,808 yards. He was also one for one for 18 yards and a touchdown pass. He played all seven years in pro ball for the Bengals. Archie was the middle of seven boys. All seven played college football!

Every now and then, you'll see one of those sports studio guys give a score like 54–0 or 34–3. These are games that you didn't see because, well, the networks switched coverage as soon as the game became a rout. One game that was played in its entirety got out of hand . . .

DECEMBER 8, 1940

The Chicago Bears scored 11 touchdowns in routing the Washington Redskins 73–0 in the NFL championship game, the first NFL championship game broadcast on radio. Red Barber called the action to 120 stations of the Mutual Broadcasting System, which paid $2,500 for the rights. The Bears intercepted eight passes in this game, returning three for touchdowns. Ten different players scored touchdowns. All three interception returns for touchdowns happened in the third quarter. Three weeks earlier, Washington had beaten Chicago 7–3 at home. After that four-point win, Redskins founder George Preston Marshall called the Bears "quitters" and "crybabies." He came to regret those remarks. George Halas named Chicago "the Bears" on January 28, 1922. He considered naming the team "the Cubs" but noted that football players are much bigger than baseball players, so if baseball players are Cubs, then football players must be Bears! The team colors have always been blue and orange as they are at Halas's alma mater, the University of Illinois.

Anytime you're with people over 55, you talk about Joe Montana being <u>the man</u>. They talk about Johnny Unitas. He was "their" quarterback.

DECEMBER 11, 1960

Johnny Unitas, quarterback for the Baltimore Colts, had his consecutive-games streak of throwing a touchdown in 47 games snapped. The Colts lost this game 10–3 to the Rams. The streak dated back to 1956. A three-time NFL MVP, Unitas was inducted into the Pro Football Hall of Fame in 1979. He was drafted in the ninth round of the 1955 NFL draft by Pittsburgh. Unitas was cut by the Steelers and got a job running a pile driver and was playing for the Bloomfield, New Jersey, Rams for $6 a game. A fan recommended him to the Baltimore Colts, and the rest is history. Unitas began his quarterbacking career with the Colts, throwing an interception that was returned for a touchdown by J. C. Caroline of the Chicago Bears on October 21, 1956. Unitas ended his career with 40,239 passing yards and 290 touchdowns.

Great games? Inevitably, after watching a nail-biter that maybe came down to a touchdown with three seconds left on the clock, somebody will say, "That was the greatest game I ever saw." "Not so fast," you'll say . . .

DECEMBER 28, 1958

At Yankee Stadium in New York in an NFL game that helped popularize the sport, Baltimore Colts fullback

Alan "The Horse" Ameche scored on a one-yard run through a huge hole in the left side of the defense, giving the Colts a 23–17 sudden death win over the New York Giants. This was an NFL championship game. Some have called it the greatest game in NFL history. The Colts had a 14–3 lead late in the third quarter and were en route to another score when the Giants stuffed Ameche on fourth down at the Giant one. New York then scored touchdowns on its next two possessions to take a 17–14 lead. With 1:56 left, Baltimore took over at its own 14. Behind quarterback Johnny Unitas and receiver Raymond Berry, they drove downfield, and Steve Myhra's 20-yard field goal with seven seconds left tied it up. In overtime, New York won the toss and elected to receive. The Colts stopped the Giants on downs, and Don Chandler punted the ball back to Baltimore. The Colts then marched 80 yards in 13 plays to win it. Who kicked New York's lone field goal? Pat Summerall.

Add this one to your O.J. file. Don't tell it around Marcia Clark, but do tell it around football fans.

DECEMBER 16, 1973

Buffalo Bills running back O. J. Simpson ran for 200 yards in a win over the New York Jets, giving him 2,003 yards for the season. It was the final game that the great Jets coach Weeb Ewbank would work. Weeb retired after 20 years of coaching football in the pros. He was the only coach to win championships in both the NFL and AFL, with the Jets and the Giants. With 6:28 left in the game, Simpson broke the 2,000-yard barrier with a seven-yard run. Eric Dickerson broke Simpson's record in 1984, rushing for 2,105 yards for the L.A.

Rams. Dickerson's record came in a 16-game season. Simpson's Buffalo squad played 14 games in 1973. Sort of like the Ruth-Maris home run record debate. Maris played in a 162-game season, Ruth in 154.

Simpson, out of USC, was Buffalo's first pick in the 1969 draft. In 1970, the Bills took O.J.'s good friend Al Cowlings, also from USC, in the first round. Cowlings played three seasons with Simpson in Buffalo. Simpson closed out his career in 1979, playing for his hometown San Francisco 49ers. Cowlings also played on that '79 49ers squad. Simpson holds the NFL record for most career games at 200-plus yards rushing with six. Three of those six games took place during the 1973 season. Walter Payton holds the NFL record for most rushing yards in a game with 275 against Minnesota on November 20, 1977.

If somebody in the room asks, "What's O.J. doing these days?" order another drink, and, as you're putting extra ice in it, go to the last day of 1967— and the Coldest Game.

DECEMBER 31, 1967

In a game played in 13-below-zero and –48-degree wind-chill conditions at Green Bay's Lambeau Field, the Packers beat Dallas 21–17 in the NFL championship game. Dallas had taken a 17–14 lead on the first play of the fourth quarter when Cowboys halfback Dan Reeves hit receiver Lance Rentzel on a 50-yard halfback option touchdown pass. Packers cornerback Bob Jeter got burned on the play. Green Bay won it with 13 seconds left when quarterback Bart Starr went in from one yard out behind guard Jerry Kramer, capping a 12-play, 68-yard drive.

The "Ice Bowl" was the Packers' third straight NFL championship. Kramer became famous because of his block on Dallas's Jethro Pugh. The Packers had no time-outs left and trailed by three. Had the Packers been stopped on Starr's sneak, they would not have been able to stop the clock and in all likelihood would have lost. Coach Vince Lombardi's call worked. Packer center Ken Bowman did more of the blocking on the play according to Pugh, the guy who should know. Kramer got credit, Bowman did a great job.

The famous instant replay of Starr's sneak almost didn't happen. CBS and Pat Summerall thought the Packers would try a rollout pass, so CBS had a camera in each end zone to isolate one on each Packer receiver. CBS's director told the cameraman behind the Cowboys to focus on receiver Boyd Dowler. One problem was that the cables behind the camera were frozen and the cameraman couldn't turn it so he had to leave it behind the Dallas defense. As it turned out, that was the best angle. What a lucky break. Viewers could see a complete breakdown of the touchdown.

Having a bad day in December? Not as bad as the Tampa Bay Buccaneers had in 1977. In fact, they had 26 bad ones.

DECEMBER 11, 1977

The Tampa Bay Buccaneers in their second NFL season finally won a game, snapping an 0–26 start. Twenty-six straight losses is still an NFL record. The Bucs went 0–14 in 1976, losing their first two games without scoring a point. Dave Green's 39-yard field goal in game three were Tampa Bay's first regular-season points. Their first-ever win was a 33–14 victory at New Orleans. In their first 26 losses, Tampa

Bay failed to score a point eleven times! The Bucs brought three interceptions back for touchdowns in their first NFL win, which tied a then NFL record. Four by Seattle in 1984 is the current record. Remarkably, behind quarterback Doug Williams, the Bucs made it to the NFC title game in 1979, which, on January 6, 1980, they lost 9–0 to the Rams.

By the way, in your great games file you can fool your friends with the greatest game played in Wrigley Field in Chicago. They will say, "Yeah, baseball in December." You'll then ask . . .

DECEMBER 17, 1933

Who won the first official NFL championship game? The Chicago Bears beat the New York Giants, 23–21. Chicago's Bill Karr scored the eventual game-winning touchdown for the Bears. The game was played at Chicago's Wrigley Field. Karr scored Chicago's last two touchdowns. Bears rookie Jack Manders kicked three field goals.

There's a continuing argument over who was better, Joe Montana or Terry Bradshaw. Both have four Super Bowl rings. Both had terrific careers. Montana had Jerry Rice. Bradshaw had the "Immaculate Reception."

DECEMBER 23, 1972

With 22 seconds left in this AFC play-off game at Pittsburgh, the Steelers were down 7–6 on their own 40 on fourth down. Terry Bradshaw rifled a pass downfield to Frenchy Fuqua. The ball, Fuqua, and Oakland Raiders safety Jack Tatum all arrived at once. The ball bounced backward to Steelers running back Franco Harris who took it in for the touchdown. Afer a long delay by the officials, the play was ruled a touchdown.

Why the delay? A ball bouncing off an offensive player to a teammate is considered an incomplete pass. Did it hit off Fuqua directly back to Harris? Also, did the ball graze the turf before Harris grabbed it and took it in? Pittsburgh then lost to Miami the next week, and two weeks later the Dolphins beat Washington in Super Bowl VII to complete a 17–0 perfect season.

New Year's Eve 1972 wasn't a celebration for everyone. Just like the day the music died when Buddy Holly went down in a plane crash with the Big Bopper and Ritchie Valens, this was the day that a big part of baseball, if not its soul, died.

DECEMBER 31, 1972

Pittsburgh Pirates outfielder Roberto Clemente was killed in a plane crash while on his way to earthquake-stricken Nicaragua to deliver supplies. Clemente finished his career with exactly 3,000 hits. His final hit was a double off Mets pitcher Jon Matlack at Three Rivers Stadium on September 30, 1972.

Clemente won 12 Gold Glove Awards, 12 years in a row, and four National League batting crowns and finished his career with a .317 average. After Clemente's death, the Baseball Hall of Fame waived the five-year mandatory waiting period and Clemente was inducted in 1973. Clemente hit safely in all seven games of both the 1960 (in which noted glove man Bill Mazeroski became a home run hero) World Series and the 1971 World Series (Clemente was named MVP of that series against Baltimore). A right fielder, Clemente was known for his very strong throwing arm.

Not many people talk about basketball in December, except, of course, you, who by now are an expert on the whole deal.

DECEMBER 13, 1983

In the high altitude of Denver, the Nuggets and Detroit Pistons combined for 370 points in the highest scoring NBA game ever. Detroit won, 186–184, in *triple* overtime! Isiah Thomas led the winners with 47 points. Denver's Kiki Vandeweghe (51) and Alex English (47) combined for 98 points in the loss. The game lasted 3 hours and 11 minutes. The most remarkable stat? Only two three-point field goals were made, one by Thomas and one by Richard Anderson. Just four were attempted. The two teams did combine for 117 free-throw attempts. The 9,655 fans at McNichol's Arena got their money's worth.

DECEMBER 16, 1961

Philadelphia Warriors big man Wilt Chamberlain began a streak of scoring 50 or more points in seven straight games as he netted exactly 50 against the Chicago Packers. He would go on to average, yes, average, 50.4 points a game on the season. He also found time to grab 25.7 rebounds a game that season.

Just in case somebody dares to try and trip you up with a pre-Christmas tennis story . . .

DECEMBER 5, 1984

Nineteen-year-old Helena Sukova beat Martina Navratilova 1–6, 6–3, 7–5 in the semifinals of the Australian Open, snapping Navratilova's record 74-match winning streak. Chris Evert Lloyd went on to beat Sukova in the finals. Navratilova also had 58- and 54-match win streaks in her great career.

ABOUT THE AUTHOR

PAT O'BRIEN is the cohost of the entertainment news show *Access Hollywood*. He has been a commentator in the world of sports for seventeen years and has hosted such events as the Winter Olympics, the Super Bowl, the NBA Finals, the NCAA Final Four tournament, the U.S. Open tennis tournament, and the World Series, as well as NBA and Major League Baseball All-Star games. Pat can be heard daily on the CBS Radio Network. He lives in Los Angeles with his wife and son, but his heart is always in South Dakota.